Chávez, Venezuela and the
New Latin America

Chávez, Venezuela and the New Latin America

An interview with Hugo Chávez
by Aleida Guevara

Cover design by ::maybe

ISBN 10: 1-920888-00-4
ISBN 13: 978-1-920888-00-8
Library of Congress Catalog Card No: 2005925581
First Printed 2005
Printed in Canada

Published in Spanish as *Chávez: Un hombre que anda por ahí* (ISBN 1-920888-22-5)

PUBLISHED BY OCEAN PRESS
Australia: GPO Box 3279, Melbourne, Victoria 3001, Australia
           Fax: (61-3) 9329 5040 Tel: (61-3) 9326 4280
           E-mail: info@oceanbooks.com.au
USA: PO Box 1186, Old Chelsea Stn., New York, NY 10113-1186, USA
           Tel: (1-212) 260 3690

OCEAN PRESS DISTRIBUTORS
United States and Canada: **Consortium Book Sales and Distribution**
           Tel: 1-800-283-3572   www.cbsd.com
Australia and New Zealand: **Palgrave Macmillan**
           E-mail: customer.service@macmillan.com.au
UK and Europe: **Pluto Books**
           E-mail: pluto@plutobooks.com
Cuba and Latin America: **Ocean Press**
           E-mail: oceanhav@enet.cu

ocean

www.oceanbooks.com.au
info@oceanbooks.com.au

For Grandmother Rosa, because her grandson still loves her

Contents

Acknowledgments

To Ocean Press for putting its trust in me to undertake this adventure.

To the Che Guevara Studies Center for its support and particularly to its principal researcher, Dr. María del Carmen Ariet, who devoted hours of intense work to helping prepare this book. It would have been practically impossible to publish without her.

To my comrades at work and to my family for the support and patience they have given me.

To President Hugo Chávez, of course, for his kindness in welcoming us and answering our questions with the spontaneity and honesty he is renowned for.

And to his brother, Adán Chávez, for his explanations and clarifications.

In short, to our people for making our dreams come true.

Preface

Aleida Guevara

Dear readers, for the first time ever I have tried to write up a conversation, and it has been a huge challenge. Though I am generally a good conversationalist, I have never written on this scale before. And, of course, we rarely manage to convey via the printed word what others have said using gesture and emotion. Have I lived up to this major challenge? Only your patience can assuage my concerns.

It is logical to ask why I have done this if I lack the experience? I cannot fully answer the question. This project developed on the basis of an idea of the publishing house Ocean Press, to make a documentary about the Bolivarian process in which the Bolivarian people and their leaders would speak. The documentary was to be made in such a way that the voices of those building a different Venezuela could be heard, and that it would counteract the lies and distortions spread about this process. In addition, Ocean Press was determined to publish a book based on the conversation I was to hold with President Chávez for the documentary. I liked the idea.

I was to some extent already acquainted with Chávez's life and personality, but it is always fascinating to learn more about a human being who has decided to transform society. This is particularly so when the transformation, aiming to improve the life of a people, defies the powerful economic interests prevailing in the world. What motivates him? What experiences have driven him to act as he has?

How do his actions reflect his own tenderness, anger, dismay? A lot of questions and very little time. The challenge was enormous, but as people in my country say, there is nothing worse than backing away from a challenge. So, on we go!

As is occasionally the case in our Latin cultures, there was a "tiny" mix-up regarding the dates of our trip, and we found ourselves on a plane bound for Caracas very suddenly. Things had presumably been organized for the interview but, surprise surprise, no one knew about our arrival. This misunderstanding was quickly cleared up and we began our acquaintance with the people: friends and enemies in this amalgamation that is the contemporary reality in Venezuela.

I will not weary you with the details, but I would like to say that from the outset I was aware that I had much to learn and that, above all, I would have to be patient. I am a pediatrician, and I presumed I had learned endurance, but I found out that patience is not enough to deal with the many lies spread by enemies of the Bolivarian process. I saw for myself that since their economic interests were affected, they were not supportive of change. And there is no doubt that, for the first time, this nation has begun to enjoy that which belongs to it by right. This much, at least, has to be acknowledged. I asked myself if anyone could legitimately deny the right to education or to health that we are due by birth. How can we carry forward projects that benefit the entire population if we do not have the financial resources required to meet these goals? Does anyone know how to do it differently? It is wise to be open to all approaches, but it is evident that in order to bring about a solution, to provide a dignified life for those who have been forgotten and exploited for centuries, the wealth of "Our America" has to be fully utilized.

On February 2 we were invited to Miraflores Palace, the Venezuelan government headquarters, where President Chávez was to speak in commemoration of his inauguration. I want to point out here an extraordinary fact: he is a president who has been "mandated" more than five times and yet attempts to undermine his legitimacy and the undeniable popularity that he enjoys persist.[1]

I saw him that day for the first time. Barely a few feet separated us when he came out to greet people at the event. But it was for only a split second: things become a little crazy when Venezuelans are up close to him — everyone wants to touch him and talk to him — and in the confusion and chaos I fell flat on my back right in the middle of the lawn. Needless to say, Chávez remained oblivious to the incident. Later on, my companions took it on themselves to remind me of how clumsy I had been to fall on my rear on the grass; it is a pity we don't have photos in order to share the moment with you. Still, it was wonderful to be there. Initially, seats were set out for guests and many people were behind us on the other side of the railings. Later, instructions were given to store away the chairs and open the doors of the palace to allow everyone in. I recalled my father's words about the people being the only sovereign we serve, and imagined him smile. It is great to be actively, directly, involved in the measures being taken by a popularly elected government.

On February 4 — an important day in the contemporary history of Venezuela [the anniversary of Chávez's first attempt to take power in 1992] — we again had the honor of being part of the celebrations. I should point out that there were two marches that day: one was joyful, with music and singing; the other was a mournful procession of the national oligarchy. The latter was very small, but it was distressing nonetheless; distressing because it demonstrated how certain self-serving interests have threatened to undermine a legitimate and sovereign process and caused a split in the country. You will have guessed, no doubt, which march we were with, and you will have been correct: we were together with those who are full of joy and hope for a better world.

That day, I finally met Chávez for just a few minutes. An aide introduced us: "This is Aleida Guevara, Mr. President." He asked me when I had arrived; I told him the previous Saturday. He replied quickly, "No, you have been here longer." "No," I answered, "Since Saturday, Mr. President." He looked at me with pleasure, saying, "You have always been here." It was a special moment, not just because a man of his stature had said such a thing, but because I realized that the one who had always been there was my father, Che.

We confirmed the day of our interview for the following Saturday, and waited.

Introduction
"Saturday, February 7, 2004"

"This is a different Venezuela, where the wretched of the earth
know that they can free themselves from their past.
And this is a different Latin America."
— Hugo Chávez, May 2004

We arrived at Miraflores Palace in the afternoon, and were informed that the conversation would be held in the presidential house, where we then headed.

We arrived as the sun was setting and discovered that the president had just completed a four-hour interview, also in front of cameras. Naturally we were concerned, thinking Chávez would be extremely tired. Time, as always, was not on our side.

What should we do? We had two projects: a documentary about the Bolivarian process that required relatively short, sharp answers regarding the history and contemporary reality of the country; and a book, for which we had more time. We decided to record some material for the documentary and suggested a second interview in order to complete the book.

The biggest problem was my lack of experience in front of a camera; I had prepared a series of roughly chronological questions, hoping to gain an insight into the development of this human being, President Hugo Chávez. I believe this was only partially accomplished.

I have chosen to organize this text just as it was communicated to me. To ensure that the text reads fluently, I have removed my questions and replaced them with thematic subtitles. I hope that by reading our fairly informal dialogue, you are able get to know this man and accept him into your hearts, just as I have done.

We prepared the set: two chairs and a tranquil courtyard, its silence interrupted only by the warbling of a solitary bird I couldn't glimpse. It seemed to be seeking our attention, which the poor thing never received. Alexandra, our cameraperson, was very nervous; it was probably the first time she had ever filmed a president. As she prepared the lights, helped by Sierra, another wonderful member of our team, I talked to Alex to calm her. It worked and she did her job as the great professional she is. When we watched the recording later, the framing was wonderful, the image quiet and sharp, and the sound clear.

After a few minutes, with everything ready, the president entered carrying his five-month-old grandson in his arms. I couldn't resist and took the child in my arms; he was beautiful. In the company of his eldest daughter and another grandchild, we began to talk.

I remember a comment he made then, recalling a question that was put to him during a TV appearance:

> Comandante, say, "This is TV!" And stupidly I said, "This is TV."
> The TV channel then transmitted this like some kind of advertising slogan.

Wasting no more time, I will begin with Chávez's analysis of what is envisaged as the new Venezuela and how the need to bring about change emerged.

Part One:
Venezuela Today

"Exorcising ourselves from Bolívar's curse"

The necessity of a new Venezuela is the outcome of many factors. Above all, this need to bring about change has emerged from developing conditions and experiences, and from my personal growth.

I became a soldier at 17, and by the age of 21, I had acquired a certain level of consciousness. To give you a better idea, I must raise certain historical facts.

Firstly, how did they come to expel Bolívar from this country, from Venezuela? When I learned this fact I couldn't believe it, I didn't want to believe it. We had always been told about Simón Bolívar, "The Liberator." Nevertheless, they threw him out. By "they" I don't mean the Spanish; it was in fact the Venezuelan oligarchy that expelled him. That same oligarchy murdered Marshal Sucre when he was only 25 years old. They expelled Bolívar's wife, Manuela Sáenz, they expelled Simón Rodríguez and all other Bolivarians, and made themselves lords of the land. It was then that Bolívar said, "I have ploughed the sea."[1]

Just a month before his death, Bolívar returned to Cartagena after almost 20 years on the battlefield. He found the city full of beggar children and asked General Mantilla, the governor of Cartagena, "What good has this damn independence done anyway?"

In the 20th century, Venezuela became a country rich with oil and resources of every description, but it was also full of poverty — a rich country full of poor people. We were soldiers in an army that was directly descended from Bolívar's United Liberation Army of South America. We had been told since we were kids, or child soldiers, that we were the heirs to Bolívar's glory.

But we soon realized they were using us to massacre our own people, who were in the streets demanding justice and protesting against the "electro-shock" therapy of the International Monetary Fund (IMF). That is when the "Caracazo" massacre occurred and Bolívar's curse fell upon us. Bolívar had once said, "Damned is the soldier who uses his weapon against his own people." After the Caracazo I said to my comrades, "We have been cursed, and we must exorcise that curse from our consciences." Three years later, we rose up in the February 4 rebellion, and the curse was lifted.

So the need for a new Venezuela emerged amid a whole series of circumstances, including factors born out of this country's prevalent corruption. Here in Venezuela, there had once been a great plan. Almost 200 years ago a plan transcended national borders: it was Bolívar's plan for a United America, a Greater Colombia, but it came to nothing. What is happening today, Aleida, is exactly what Neruda predicted when he said, "Bolívar wakes every 100 years when the people awake."

The culmination of these historical factors — the collapse of that plan, the abuse of an entire people, and the awakening of a popular consciousness among civilians and patriotic soldiers — has been the birth of a new Venezuela.

After February 4, 1992, I was imprisoned for two years and two months. I learned a lot during that period. Prison is a kind of a school; you develop a soul of steel, your convictions are strengthened, and your awareness is deepened. Looking at it from an ideological perspective, throughout all those days and nights in prison, we were prisoners of conscience, prisoners with dignity, prisoners who knew exactly why we were there.

In 1987 as a second lieutenant in the plains region I was always reading and thinking. One event signified a great learning curve for me: reading Plekhanov's *The Role of the Individual in History*. At that time I began to develop an awareness of the idea of necessity. If you are aware that you serve a purpose within a larger scheme, whatever that purpose might be, it doesn't matter if you are thrown into a dungeon. You remain free. You are free because you are playing your part. And it is vital that you do so. While in prison, those thoughts and readings from years before came to mind, and I never felt trapped, I never felt desperate or even imprisoned. I felt free, even in that tiny space, and I made the most of my time — from an ideological point of view. All that we had studied over the years could be absorbed to a great degree. And a Bolivarian ideology began to take root. Bolívar is not just a man, Bolívar is a concept. More than just a theory, Bolívar is a complex set of ideas related to politics, society, and justice. These ideas remain relevant to the national, South American, Caribbean, and world arenas, because Bolívar engendered an international idea. He spoke of what today we call a multipolar world.

He proposed the unification of South and Central America into what he called Greater Colombia, to enable negotiations on an equal basis with the other three quarters of the globe. This was his multipolar vision.

Bolívar was also anti-imperialist. He said to a general friend of his, for example, "The United States seems destined by providence to infest America with misery in the name of liberty."

Through our studies and discussions in prison we developed a new approach, which later we took to the streets as the doctrine of the Bolivarian Fifth Republic Movement (MVR). We discussed the Bolivarian project: strategies to bring about the transformation of one situation to another, how to overcome obstacles, and effect radical change. In this way the idea of a constituent assembly, which as an idea was just a seedling on February 4, grew tall and strong in prison. We deepened our analysis of the French Revolution's original concept of a revolutionary constituent power — the power of the people.

We spent our time in prison broadening and consolidating our thinking. I remember when I was released on March 26 a group of journalists stopped me as I came out of the military fort in Caracas. One of them asked me, "And where are you going now?" I answered, "To power." Just like that, in two words, "To power." You see, we came out of prison with much clearer ideas, more focused and spiritually strengthened, and above all we were released into the realm of the most wonderful thing: a warm and welcoming public.

In February 4, 1992, we had a basic strategic plan to overthrow the government and convene a constituent assembly. When other soldiers asked us what we would do next, we replied quite naïvely: we will establish a real constituent power and return to our barracks. I admit this was rather naïve, we were only kids after all, quixotic kids. We were a bit like that other Don Quixote when he said, "Once again I feel beneath my heels the ribs of Rocinante."[2] Considering our desperation in the circumstances, perhaps this was natural. But we had our ideas and, of course, with the help of left-wing figures and civil leaders we had already drawn up a series of decrees. One such figure was Cléver Ramírez, a veteran guerrilla fighter.

We were in touch with what was known as Causa R,[3] but in the end they backed away, because our idea was more profound than a military rebellion. Our concept was civil-military; it had always been that way. It involved the participation of the working class. Yesterday I was talking with some workers' leaders: with Ramón Machuca, from Causa R, who has been with us since the beginning, as was Alfredo Maneiro, an ex-guerilla leader who unfortunately died young.[4] I recalled that in meetings prior to February 4 we had already begun an orientation process; we were already talking about workers' battalions. We envisioned that on the day of the rebellion the entire population would be in the street, with people, workers, and soldiers taking up arms.

Because of the way events unfolded this didn't happen, but the project — to convene a constituent assembly and allow the country to continue its democratic development after making a clean break with the Fourth Republic — still remained.

We developed this idea much more during the two years in prison and we were much wiser by the time we got out. Well, not all of us, because some came out and joined the ranks of Caldera's government.[5] But those of us who decided to go on fighting for our Bolivarian beliefs came out of prison stronger and more focused.

On February 4, 1992, I was a lieutenant colonel, which is what I remained. We wore our uniforms in prison. They wanted to take them off us, but we refused. After I was released I asked to be relieved from duty, because it didn't make any sense to return to the army and the barracks.

Origins

On my father's side I have a mixture of indigenous and African blood, of which I am very proud. For me, being indigenous means being part of the deepest and most authentic roots of our people and our land. And the mix works well, like in the case of Cubans. Last year I met a Cuban athlete, who was here teaching sport to young Venezuelans. I was awarding her a certificate of appreciation for her work. She was very beautiful — black with light-colored eyes. We got talking and she said, "You Venezuelans and we Cubans are the perfect blend: indigenous, African, and a touch of white as well."

Yes, I feel very proud. I'm aware that when I look at our people I see the result of the colonial collision — the invasion here in Venezuela and in Santo Domingo, Cuba, and the rest of the Caribbean by the Spanish, together with the English and the Portuguese, who all devastated the region. All these factors stir our consciences and open our eyes as we grow into adults. I was already a soldier when I began to think about these things and started to wake up.

When I was in high school I was only interested in playing baseball and being a pitcher in the Major League or with the Magallanes. I dreamed of being a professional baseball player. I didn't enter military academy because I wanted to be a soldier, but because that was the only way I could get to Caracas. We were very poor and my father couldn't afford to pay the school fees in Caracas. So I finished high school and entered the academy, planning to stay for just a year and then leave to play baseball.

I learned what happened to the indigenous people by studying history, by reading. After reading Frei Bartolomé de las Casas and other history books, I saw what had really happened. They slaughtered us. This knowledge often brought me into conflict with the life I was leading. When we were cadets they used to make us march past a statue of Columbus in front of the hospital. I used to ask my comrades, "Why on earth should we pay tribute to the man who launched the invasion?" It was really too much.

It has taken 30 years to bring us, and our people, to power, to begin this new phase and put things in their proper place. The statue? We didn't pull Christopher Columbus down, he's still standing there, but we don't pay tribute to him anymore. Now we honor Guaicaipuru, leader of the indigenous resistance. Just before the Spanish killed him, after killing his wife and children, Guaicaipuru shouted a challenge to the Spanish saying, "Come, Spaniards, and see how an Indian, a free man of this land, Guaicaipuru, can die." We honor the indigenous chiefs Manau, Aimar, Tabacares, the Caribbean Indians — "*Ana Karina Rote auno toto paparoto mantoro.*" [Cry of the native Caribbean people: "We are the only men. The others are our slaves."] When I say these words I feel the Caribbean stirring within me, because I am Indian, mixed with African, with a touch of white thrown in. We are not anti-white racists!

The concept of a people should always be a concrete reality, not an abstraction. But the abstraction often rules. For a people to exist there should be a common consciousness among the inhabitants of a common territory, sharing a common history. The people should drink from a common fountain and, above all, share a common social project.

So when you ask about the Venezuelan people, there are numerous ways this can be understood, depending on the era to which you refer. There was a time when our people were not really a people. There was no understanding of our past, we didn't drink from one fountain, shared no ideas, and were manipulated and tricked time and time again.

That was "their" time... As a young boy, certain things used to make me sad. Those *miameros*, for example, middle-class Venezuelans who couldn't wait to get to Miami on vacation, saying, "That's cheap, I'll take two, look at these clothes, they're cheap, give me two..." Venezuela was famous around the world for its wealthy spendthrifts, its beautiful women, and its oil. But the real Venezuela is where you are now, where the people have acquired a deep awareness of the world, Aleida, so deep it's incredible. Perhaps this anecdote I'd like to tell you might capture the essence of this people who have been abused and exploited for 200 years.

Last year, in the middle of the oil strike — what we called "the oil terror" — the Venezuelan establishment and their international allies sabotaged the oil refineries, threw away millions of liters of milk, and slaughtered cattle so there would be no food. Their plan was to produce social meltdown, chaos, and collapse. There was no petrol, no natural gas, almost no food, although we had been making huge efforts in all areas. I remember Fidel sent us a ship full of beans, telling me over the phone, "Pay whenever you can." Other goods came from Brazil. We brought milk, meat, and petrol from Colombia. In those days people would have to wait three or four days in long lines to buy a few liters of fuel.

On one of those difficult afternoons, I told some of my comrades I wanted to see for myself what was going on up there in the hills. So a small group of us went up. There was a lot of activity in the streets, people searching for a little rice, a few bananas. We were walking around and people started to greet us. I was talking to them, asking them how they were, when a strong, old, black woman grabbed me by the hand and yanked me over saying, "Come here, Chávez!"

There was no arguing with her! "Come here, Chávez, follow me, I want you to see my house." We walked up some steps and they were cooking rice, potatoes, and plantains in a pan over firewood. The old woman looked deep into my eyes and grabbed me by the lapels, "Chávez, I've got no chairs left in my house. That firewood you see burning are the legs off the bed. We'll burn the furniture, the roof, and we'll even break down the doors and cook with them, but don't you dare give in Chávez." The three million people who have realized what we are doing in this country share that woman's conviction. This is really not so remarkable. You asked, "What is the essence of the Venezuelan people?" They are a warrior people, a battalion. Bolívar once said that Venezuela was born in the middle of a military campaign. An entire people went to war, a people became an army: men, women, and even children were ready to sacrifice themselves against the Spanish.

Those same people were dreamers, a nation of dreamers with Bolívar at their head. The quixotic Bolívar said, "Let's unite the whole of Latin America... the America that was once Spanish," then he took his army to Potosí. And in Ayacucho, Sucre crushed the imperialists and united the Argentines, the people of Rio del Plata, of Chile, Artigas, Panama, and he created an entire United Liberation Army, which even planned to liberate Cuba and Puerto Rico.

Our willpower has been put to the test. Our people are strong and capable of great love. And if you know the Cuban people, you already know the Venezuelan people, because, as Bolívar said, the whole of the Americas, which was once Spanish, is our homeland, and all of its people are equals.

The revolutionary process

Let's look at our revolutionary process chronologically. I've explained this process — how the decision to use electoral methods came into being — a million times in a million different places. When we were released from prison on March 26, 1994, and that journalist asked me, "Where are you going now, *comandante*?" and I answered, "To power," we were still unsure of what methods we were going to use. We really hadn't decided how to act; we were just determined to continue fighting. We have said it a thousand times: this is a peaceful revolution, even when it hasn't always been so and blood has been spilled in the streets. In general, peace has been maintained.

I once warned the Venezuelan oligarchy and the counterrevolutionaries not to make the mistake of believing that this peaceful revolution is an unarmed revolution. We are peaceful, but we are armed. With military weaponry, that is, but we also have weapons for many different battles. Our ideology, our conviction, our awareness, and our constitution are all weapons.

But back then our method of combat was not clearly defined. We spent the whole of 1994 drawing up and assessing plans. Then we came up with our war cry. In 1994 there were elections for governors and mayors; we realized that armed struggle was not at all appropriate. We began to look at ways of breaking the stranglehold of the neoliberal governors. We decided to run in the elections, put forward patriotic Bolivarian candidates, explain our ideas, and establish the

Bolivarian movement in every town and village. We traveled around the entire country. In 1995, Aleida, a year after we were released from prison, we celebrated the third anniversary of the February 4 rebellion. By that time, each of our top cadres had been imprisoned, except me. That's when I said to Caldera, "Well, come and get me, send your boys to pick me up, and let's see who lasts longer: me in prison, or you in Miraflores Palace."

We were under siege and being denigrated. They were talking about the Colombian guerrillas; about whether we would ask Fidel to help set up a "Greater Colombian" or "South American" guerrilla movement; and many other ridiculous accusations. But against hell and high water we built our revolutionary movement, the Fifth Republic Movement (MVR), town by town, city by city, neighborhood by neighborhood, in universities and factories. And like an enormous net it began to spread.

We constantly emphasized our ideology and our project, our strategic trajectory, and our ideas. We have constantly done this since then. We have always adhered to our strategic map, which I know by heart and will never forget, having explained it so many times in so many different ways. We drew this map in the sand; we went into indigenous villages in the jungle and to miners' camps. There wasn't a single corner of the country we didn't visit during 1994, 1995, and 1996, all the time analyzing and evaluating the process.

In 1997 the debate on the methods we would use to take us to power reopened. The 1998 elections were looming. The polls, manipulated by the establishment, predicted Irene Sáenz would be elected president, with 60 percent popularity. She's an ex-Miss Universe: a very beautiful woman who was mayor of Chacao. We could also say that she was their last chance, their final hope. Whose hope? The hope of a dying social class.

On February 4, [1992], Caldera was the only political leader who did not condemn our rebellion outright. He said that when people are hungry they do not defend democracy. That wily old fox was only saying what the public wanted to hear. He arose from among the political dead and two years later [in 1993] he was elected president. But in the end he sank the ship, or at least condemned its crew, because he was one of the founders of the Punto Fijo project.[6]

So the local establishment and their international allies backed Irene Sáenz. They helped prepare her and in all the polls, she was unbeatable. Two years before the 1998 elections, Irene Sáenz had 80 percent of the vote. And what about Hugo Chávez? I used to watch those programs on TV, but I was never asked to appear. I was silenced — on the TV, the radio, and in the print media. Certain journalists were sacked for broadcasting a recorded interview with me on the radio. They closed down any stations that interviewed me. I was totally censored.

One night I was watching a TV program where the chances of each electoral candidate were being discussed: Irene Sáenz 77 percent, Claudio Fermín 10 percent. Someone in the studio asked, "What about Chávez? Your poll doesn't mention *comandante* Chávez." The commentator replied, "No, no, he is just a myth that has evaporated." That made me laugh because I was out there in the streets and I knew the impact we were having, not me personally, but the movement and the Bolivarian project.

We feared that that they would try to cheat us; that our money would run out. Sometimes someone would ask me, "Chávez, how are we going to pay the bills?"

"I don't know," I would respond.

"How are we going to run our campaign against these millionaires who control the media?"

"I don't know how, and I don't know with what, but we will do it." This is the way forward, I would tell them.

They ran campaigns to paint me as "Chávez the crazy man!" They said this over and over again, "That Chávez is insane!" "Have you heard the latest about Chávez? Before dinner he puts on his military dress uniform, sits at the table, and is served by his wife. But he always leaves the chair at the head of the table empty because it's Simón Bolívar's chair. He even gets them to make food for Bolívar!" That's what they were saying. They also said I had commandeered a squad from the Colombian army to kill anyone in my way and that this squad had once killed eight Venezuelan soldiers. These lies spread to Colombia and the Colombian president, who then sent a letter to the president here about the "incident." They did all this and more. Imagine the frenzy of the press and radio and TV commentators!

They circulated millions of flyers throughout the country that said, "Chávez is a traitor." They painted red slogans in the streets of Caracas saying, "Chávez traitor, Chávez traitor." When I went to Havana [after getting out of prison] they filled the front pages of the newspapers with photos of me embracing Fidel. They dug all this up again during the [1998] electoral campaign, even though it had happened back in 1994. They had experts on TV analyzing the footage of Fidel accompanying me to the steps of the airplane. I was dressed in civilian clothes but wearing my olive green *liquiliqui* and a red beret.[7] We saluted each other when we said good-bye. Do you know what they did? They slowed the image and the expert said, "Watch carefully, Fidel Castro salutes and then lowers his hand, while Chávez keeps his hand raised. In semiotics and military symbolism, this means that Chávez is under Fidel Castro's command."

They even hired a professional actor to imitate my voice, who did so incredibly well! They took him to a studio and recorded his voice as though he was giving a speech saying, "I'm going to fry the heads of those *adecos* and *copeyanos* in oil."[8] They imposed his voice over footage of me in a meeting, as if I were saying those words. I saw it and thought, "Hey! That's my voice, but I didn't say that! That voice is exactly like mine, my god! I didn't say that, I'm not that mad, I did not say that!" Everyone thought that I had said those things, even some of my supporters believed it, even though I told them, "I did not say that, do you hear me?" But then the actor came forward and said that he had been lied to; he had been told they were making a comedy and he had been paid I don't know how many million bolívars.[9] But he denounced their lie. He said he had been tricked and had imitated my voice; that the voice wasn't mine. This was of course a blow to the opposition.

We started down the electoral path and in the end, despite their predictions and deceptions, came December 6, 1998, a victory for our wise people.

But in answer to your question about what we did after coming to power: I have told you that I had said so many times, we will go to Miraflores Palace, go to government, and convene a constituent assembly. That this was the only way to bring down the Fourth Republic and allow a Fifth Republic to be born. That we must build a bridge between the former situation we are still trying to fully free ourselves from, and march toward a new national situation. That this will be the final split; a watershed. But of course that requires the empowerment of constituent forces. After coming to power I was often asked, "Now that you are president, how will you achieve that?"

"I'll call a referendum." Many people said this was anti-constitutional and that it couldn't be done. Nevertheless, I said we should try, we must try. On constitutional grounds and according to the law of suffrage, referendums could be called. Of course, no one had ever done it before and it didn't appear explicitly in the constitution. People therefore said it couldn't be done. But there was an article regarding referendums buried in a law, and I clung to that. I also pointed to article 4 of the old constitution, which stated: "Sovereignty lies with the people, who exercise it through their suffrage of the organs of public power."

There was an extremely heated legal and political debate. I came to Miraflores Palace on February 2, 1999 [for the inauguration], with, as Fidel said, a sea of people behind me, and the first thing I did was sign a decree calling a referendum.

The opposition presented 25 challenges before the Supreme Court in an attempt to annul the decree. The court took a historic decision and assumed a great responsibility. If they had ruled out the constitutional option we would have been left with no choice but to use violence. There would have been no other way. It was John F. Kennedy I think, not much of a revolutionary himself, who once said, "Those who make peaceful revolution impossible make violent revolution inevitable."

The referendum took place and we elected the Constituent Assembly. The Constituent Assembly itself was the center of another great debate; there had already been assemblies of its kind. There was one in Colombia and it didn't change anything. There was one in Ecuador but it wasn't properly established. There was one in Argentina, convened by [Carlos] Menem, but it just served to strengthen his regime and its neoliberal project.

We said, "We must create a revolutionary assembly that will unleash the pent up, transformative power from which the new Venezuela will spring." The assembly was proclaimed sovereign and plenipotentiary. In other words, it was in no way subordinate to the congress, to the Supreme Court, or to the president.

Practically everyone participated in that debate. In Washington and Europe, they asked, "Has a dictatorship reemerged?" But we had no dictatorship and no powers were dissolved. A strange thing happened here. In the parliament building both the congress that was elected in 1998, in which we were in a minority, and the Constituent Assembly, were in session at the same time, one in the right wing of the building and one in the left. These were the revolution's very first steps.

Yes, there were many conflicts. People surrounded the palace on several occasions and violence was often close to erupting. The year 1999 was fervent and tense, and a time of great debate. The new constitution was passed in 1999, which was a year dedicated to political transformation: to bringing forth the new constitution and to forging the new project. That was the first big step forward. At the same time, Aleida, as a government we were facing an inherited economic crisis. We had no money at all; the little there was they took with them when they left.

I remember our first cabinet meetings in 1999 when there really was no money. The oil price was very low due to a foolish policy that ran totally against Venezuelan interests. The oil price was around $7 a barrel, but the budget for that year had been calculated at oil being around $14 a barrel. There was no money to pay the teachers and government employees. This international oil price was the result of a US strategy to flood the market. Reagan once said, "We will bring OPEC to its knees," and that's exactly what they had done. Venezuela followed orders from Washington, and was playing the US game. Venezuela was producing more than four million barrels of oil [a day] and so the Saudis had increased their production as well. It was all-out war in the oil market. We were almost giving the oil away. It cost more to extract the oil than we received by selling it. We cut back oil production immediately.

From an economic point of view, they handed us a country in crisis. Massive external debt, low wages, inflation running at over 35 percent, almost 20 percent unemployment, generalized poverty. But our revolutionary resourcefulness came to the fore to turn the situation around. One thing we did was design Plan Bolívar 2000, in which the armed forces went to work in the streets alongside civilian volunteers. Plan Bolívar focused on the poorest sectors: repairing schools, building local markets, and providing food. It was a revolutionary civil-military effort and it had a huge impact. Plan Bolívar began on February 27, 1999, exactly 10 years after the Caracazo massacre, and was designed to restore the true role of the armed forces as servants of the people. More than 60,000 soldiers across the entire country took to the streets at 6 a.m. each day. From paratroopers to the national guards, everyone participated to help the neediest.

Transformation of the constitutional army into a people's army

We built a new army, little by little, via collective effort, the credit is not mine alone. We spent many years sowing the seeds of doubt among the ranks; we built consciousness.

Let me tell you about my personal experience. In October 1977, 23-year-old second lieutenant Hugo Chávez was in the eastern mountains. I decided to form an army, "the Bolivarian Army of the Liberation of the Venezuelan People." There were more words than members in that army.

There were five of us in total when we began our work. At that time I was reading and studying a lot, as I told you. On several occasions I even thought about leaving the [Venezuelan] army. I was very young and I felt very unhappy.

There were still guerrillas in the area. I was the officer in command of a little guard post. A colonel arrived late at night. There was a curfew in place because it was a security buffer zone and the guerrillas usually attacked at night. The colonel was only going to spend one night there. That night I saw a local farmer being tortured; the colonel was hitting the farmer with a baseball bat. Well, he wasn't actually doing the hitting; he had one of the soldiers under my command do it for him. I got into real hot water because I said to the soldier with the baseball bat, "I'll give you five seconds to get out of here. One, two, three, four..." and he ran off into the bushes. The colonel nearly blew his top, "Are you insane?" he shouted.

"Not me. What on earth are you doing up here, beating up this 'guerrilla fighter?'" The victim didn't even look anything like a guerrilla; he was just a poorly dressed farmer. Later, he was found dead nearby with some other men. They'd all been murdered. I told the colonel that night, "Either you put the prisoners of war under my charge or you leave immediately. This is not a concentration camp."

I got into trouble again in the city of Cumaná, where I had been sent to give a lecture at a teacher training college. This incident comes to mind because, a few days ago, on February 3, we were paying tribute to Marshal Sucre, who was born in Cumaná. I remembered this when we were going to the airport, and asked the governor who was beside me, "Isn't there a teacher training college here in Cumaná?" He replied that there was. I told him about the trouble I got into back in 1977, a short while before the incident in the mountains. They had sent me there to give a lecture, and I ended up speaking about Che Guevara. My superiors scratched their heads and asked, "What is a uniformed second lieutenant doing speaking to these students about Bolívar and Che Guevara in the same breath?" They summoned me immediately and demanded an explanation. They ordered me to file a report. So I wrote that my lecture was a way of studying the enemy from within, but this was a lie. I was speaking about Che in the same way I spoke about Bolívar.

This process was long and arduous and took half of the 1970s and all of the 1980s. But we were maturing all the time. In 1982 I was in the center of the country. I was a captain by then, not a child second lieutenant with five members of our Bolivarian army (which didn't last very long by the way, because I was transferred and the others, all farm boys, were released from military service). By 1982, things were very different. I was a captain in the paratroopers. We swore an oath beneath a tree, a very famous tree here in Venezuela: the *samán*, which as history records Bolívar once camped under.[10]

The huge tree is over 300 years old and we swore our oath there, pledging ourselves to the construction of a Bolivarian movement within the army.

We began to work intensely, throughout the 1980s and even up until 1992. February 4 was the culmination of this work, but the movement had been gathering strength for years. Even when we were in prison the movement within the army continued to grow, and we were released without ever having lost contact with the troops.

There is a marked difference between the generations within the movement. Until very recently, and even in the early years of the Bolivarian government, the vast majority of the armed forces commanders were from a different era. In contrast, the military leaders are now all from my generation; the majority of them are my contemporaries and comrades. General Baduel, for example, the commander-in-chief of the army, was one of those who took the oath under the *samán* in 1982. The air force commander, General Cordero, a fighter pilot, also took the oath — in an air base one long night back in the 1980s. The navy commander is the same, as well as his wife, who is a captain and has been a revolutionary for years. Not to mention the head of the national guard. All the way down the military pyramid you will find that Bolivarian ideas are everywhere.

To give you further examples, almost all today's battalion commanders joined the movement, either directly or indirectly, when they were very young. They joined a movement that fully appreciated the importance of using the military academy and main military bases as forums for debate and discussion. To create civic-minded soldiers and military-conscious civilians has always been our aim. I was a teacher in the military school for four years and my comrades there Acosta Carles, Acosta Chijín, Ronald Blanco, who is now governor of Táchira, and Edgar Hernández, current president of CADIVI,[11] who was the second lieutenant of the school, were the original core of revolutionary young people whose numbers gradually multiplied, and who are still fighting for Bolivarian principles.

On one occasion, I was posted to the [Colombian] border and was under close surveillance. They sent me out there with no troops to command. I was in a kind of wilderness, but I never relinquished my ideas and remained keenly aware of our need to struggle. "If I am here, this is where I will engage in struggle." And I knew that far away the movement was taking shape and Bolivarian ideas were gaining ground in the barracks.

On occasions I came to Caracas. I was virtually undercover. I couldn't go to the military school because that would be a black mark against my comrades, jeopardizing their safety. For basic secrecy reasons I couldn't openly contact the troops in the barracks. The top brass were monitoring me — wanting to know who I was speaking to. Wherever I went I had to try and throw them off my trail. When I came to Caracas I would go out quite openly with friends, have a drink, play softball. But late at night, I would put on a wig; can you imagine me in a wig? I would disguise myself, and would even be smuggled around in the trunk of a car, always changing my disguise, always moving around in the middle of the night.

One night I got a call from Blanco Lemus. He was a lieutenant and I was a major, and he said, "We need you. Come to the academy, we need you here, tonight. I'm on guard duty." And so the operation began. After taps, the cadets go to bed and the officers go home. Only those on duty stay awake. And in the silence, with the guards under control, I entered the academy through the kitchen door. It was a shock for the officers, because they thought I was out in the wilderness with my spirit broken. They couldn't have been more wrong; a well-developed consciousness, even in the hardest of times, allows no negativity.

I was led into the academy and told, "Come in, we've got a surprise for you, a wonderful surprise." We went to a large hall full of uniformed cadets. There were about 40 cadets and their lieutenants waiting for me. I was in civilian clothes of course. A captain gave a speech first and then asked me to speak to the young soldiers. I looked at him in amazement thinking, "Have they gone mad? Are we going to speak to so many people just like that?" But all of them were hanging on our every word. And when we finished, they took the oath, the Bolivarian oath. So you see, Aleida, Bolivarian principles had taken root.

February 4 brought together about 100 officers, a few more perhaps, from commanders down. When we were taken to prison there was really no room for all of us. We were an avalanche of well-prepared men, some of us training and teaching the rest.

The Caracazo gave our movement a great boost. I've come to believe that without the Caracazo it would have been very difficult, or at least it would have taken much longer, for the military movement to gather strength. The disaster produced this, when Bolívar's curse fell so heavily upon us. Many of us actually saw the dead bodies, and even then they tried to tell us Fidel Castro was responsible. Fidel came to Venezuela, as you know, on February 4, 1989, when Carlos Andrés Pérez took office, but the Caracazo took place 20 days later. After the Caracazo, the generals called a meeting to tell us their lies. I stood up and said, "General, who do you think we are? Where on earth did you get the idea that Fidel Castro deposited 200 Cubans in the hills of Caracas?" Yet they still said it was Fidel who had left Cubans here to stir up the people as if they were mad dogs. Can you imagine a more absurd idea?

Regardless, after the tragedy the consciousness of our soldiers was strengthened. We lost one of our commanders, Acosta Carles,[12] in the Caracazo. They killed him and we were outraged. It was a severe blow at the very heart of the movement. I'd like to tell you a story that will make it clear why it's not surprising that the Venezuelan army and the entire armed forces are now committed to social welfare projects for the benefit of the most needy. It explains just why the army, national guard, navy, and air force refused to follow the orders of the Pentagon and the traitor generals on April 11, 2002.

The forces behind the coup d'état recruited 70 generals and admirals, but they couldn't control a single battalion, except their own of course, which was a battalion of generals. The troops ultimately captured them, as they captured Carmona.[13] Not one single soldier trained his gun on a civilian that April 11, 2002.

So you can see that it is natural that the Venezuelan armed forces are now committed to the revolutionary process, to the Bolivarian project for social justice.

After the Caracazo I was working in Miraflores Palace, in the White Palace. I managed to get a post there after I left the border — and that is where, a couple of months after the massacre, I was arrested. Just a few days after the tragedy I was returning from the university, where I was taking a postgraduate course in political science. I was coming back with my books to the little room in the White Palace where I slept. A young officer approached me suddenly. I didn't know him very well. He said, "Major, I need to speak to you."

"Well, let's go to my office," I replied.

The young man said, "Major, they say you are involved in a movement. They're talking about a Bolivarian movement." Of course, I had learned to be cautious and I didn't know the kid. I feigned ignorance. "The word on the street is that you are in the movement."

"Why are you asking me this?" He told me his tragic story about how he had been ordered to patrol near the palace during the Caracazo. He detained a group of kids who were looting a shop and took them to a sports court close by; a basketball court in the neighborhood. He held them there but with no bad feeling. The kids even talked to him, "Okay, lieutenant, you can let us go now, right?"

"I'll release you soon, but you must stop looting," he warned. He told me he'd planned to release them later in the afternoon, but then an order arrived from some commission that he had to transfer them to the Tiuna fort[14] or to the DISIP headquarters.[15] He obeyed the order and handed them over to an official from DISIP, the state's secret police. They were loaded into a truck. There were about 12 or 15 kids. They even said good-bye, "See you later lieutenant, you didn't let us go after all." The lieutenant gathered his men and went back to his patrol. Half an hour later they found all those kids in an alley. They had been murdered. He wept with rage when he saw them, and protested, but was told to keep quiet, told to keep his nose out of it. He finished his story, saying, "Listen, major, if you do have a movement, tell me, because if not, I'm getting out of here." I didn't say anything that night for obvious security reasons, but I told him I was also opposed to what had happened.

Later, I gathered more information on that young man from comrades who knew him well. He joined the movement and participated in the February 4 rebellion. That's just one case. There are many others among the young soldiers.

During the terrible days of the Caracazo, people took to the streets to protest against neoliberalism, against the "electro-shock" therapy of the IMF, against universal privatization, unemployment, and hunger. They sent us soldiers to fill those people with lead. The political leaders, so-called democrats, spoke of justice and democracy. What democracy? That was not democracy, it was pure dictatorship: an oligarchic government using the armed forces and the media to brainwash and confuse the people. There was no democracy here. Democracy is only being established now, although it is not yet the democracy we dream of: a fully participatory and citizen-led democracy. In those days we had a true dictatorship, exercised through the political parties that were fighting over the spoils of the Fourth Republic.

Social welfare programs

Let's begin with the objectives [of the social welfare programs]. We have taken these directly from Bolívar, who spoke and wrote about them often. The perfect form of government is that which guarantees the greatest degree of happiness for its people. That is our objective, our central aim: to achieve the greatest happiness for all the people.

We had created a government — effectively, a political and constituent-led revolution — in the midst of massive social need. I decided to invite the unemployed to come to Miraflores Palace. They were a veritable army, and during those visits their lines circled the palace several times. They came with expectations we couldn't hope to fulfill. That was a mistake we made. The process of revolutionary government began in the middle of serious shortages. At one point we had to buy mattresses so that people outside, and even inside, the government palace could be made a little more comfortable. The poor were saying, "Chávez has arrived, let's go to Caracas to tell him about our situation." It was a virtual avalanche of poverty stricken people; I barely slept with the torment. I signed the constituent decree and the Constituent Assembly was elected.

I didn't forget about [the drafting process of the new constitution], I thought it was in the hands of the movement and the political parties. I was very busy, but perhaps if I had devoted more time we could have prevented some of the minor mistakes that occurred.

Nevertheless, the process as a whole continued to gather strength. The new constitution may have its problems that we will have to correct, but the political process and debate took their course.

Every major issue was discussed [before the new constitution was ratified]: homosexuals arrived [at the palace] to demand same-sex marriages; women's groups came to demand the right to abortion; indigenous peoples from the jungle arrived in traditional costume, playing drums, dancing, and demanding respect for their rights; black Venezuelans from Barlovento came with their drums and dances, and took over the congress. Children came and formed their own assembly. I was married at the time so they came to visit the First Lady because she worked in the social commission of the Constituent Assembly. Miraflores Palace was constantly full of people asking for things. One day the children asked for a children's convention. "We have rights; we want to participate as well." Everyone was demanding their rights, the evangelicals, the nuns, everyone!

All this anguish became a flood. I had unleashed a tide of desire for justice among the people. That was when Plan Bolívar was devised. Plan Bolívar would place the armed forces at the disposal of a state that had previously been an obstacle and a brake on society. Every single governor — except my father who against all expectations had won the elections in Barinas[16] and Manuitt in Guarico of the PPT[17] — were *adecos* and *copeyanos* opposed to us. All the mayors — except Pastora Medina of the PPT, mayor in the state of Bolívar — were *adecos* or *copeyanos*. Electoral power, judicial power, everything, was in the hands of those two parties [the Democratic Action party and the Christian Social party].

I was the head of state, but what kind of state? A ship of a state that was rapidly sinking. I came to power to sink it finally, which was why on the day of my inauguration I took the oath in a particular way. The president of the congress placed the constitution [of the

Fourth Republic] before me and asked, "Do you swear [on this constitution]?" I didn't know what to say, but I knew it had to be different from all previous presidents. Caldera was at my side, the last president of *puntofijismo*. What I suddenly thought of, what came from my heart, was practically to blaspheme in front of those decrepit *adeco* dinosaurs, and in front of Carlos Andrés Pérez (who was a senator and sitting in the front row, having been elected in the congressional elections). I said, "I swear before this waning constitution that I will do everything in my power to give our people a true Magna Carta worthy of their dreams," or something along those lines. My idea was not to swear allegiance to that constitution but rather to kill and bury it.

Returning, however, to the social sphere. We dedicated the armed forces, the ministries, and all their resources to health care. Venezuela's health system had been totally decentralized and destroyed — another neoliberal trick is decentralization.

In the field of education, schools were charging parents when they went to enroll their children. To keep your children in public school you had to pay a "voluntary" contribution, but it wasn't voluntary at all. Parents had to pay quite simply because almost nothing had been set aside in the budget for education or health. Everything was privatized; life was privatized.

In terms of housing, there were simply no housing plans. We began to take certain steps. We didn't have, and didn't want, the support of the IMF or similar organizations. We had almost nothing. We couldn't even rely on revenue from Venezuelan oil.

We began to use the little we did have and that avalanche of poor people came to ask for their wishes to be granted. People demonstrated a keen awareness [of events] and I decided to speak directly to the nation. The idea of "Aló Presidente" was born.[18] We started with another weekly TV program called "Face to Face with the President," but it didn't really take off. We also published a small informative newspaper called *El Correo del Presidente*, designed mainly to inform the public of what we were doing, of the gravity of the situation we had inherited and to ask for their patience. I've always used one of Bolívar's sayings, "Work and more work, patience and more patience, perseverance and more perseverance to govern." The people have accepted this and opinion polls show that the vast majority agree that the country's problems cannot be solved through short-term strategies.

Instead we began to implement our program, and Plan Bolívar was at the heart of social welfare projects. I began to travel the world. We visited OPEC leaders. Our main aim in those visits was to gather resources and to strengthen OPEC by cutting back on oil production. Not just our own production; we traveled to the OPEC countries to let them know that a new government had come to power in Venezuela, that we would respect the quotas, but that each of us had to reduce oil production. Our plan worked. When I arrived in Iraq I had no idea I was the first president to visit Baghdad after the 1991 Gulf War. I only found this out after Washington declared they were totally opposed to my visit to Baghdad. I told them I was going anyway; they argued that there was a no-fly zone I couldn't pass through or they might shoot down the plane. But we went to Baghdad anyway and spoke to Saddam. Then we visited Gaddafi, then to Saudi Arabia to speak with the king, then to Kuwait and Qatar. We went to Nigeria and Indonesia, across the seven seas in a 10-day tour. Speaking to all those heads of state, explaining our plan, we made progress and an OPEC summit was called.

By the end of 1999, oil was at $16 a barrel, enabling us to increase social spending despite our external debt. In our first budget of 2000 we increased education and health spending. We eliminated the enrollment charges in public schools. A tidal wave of children hit the schools; we had to convert barracks into schools. In Miraflores Palace we turned a soldiers' bunkhouse into a school, which is still there.

Other schools have remained permanently in the barracks, as is the case at the paratrooper brigade's barracks.

Simply banning enrollment fees created this avalanche of children. In September 1999 we calculated that the number of children in education would increase to 300,000 and we started to repair the schools.

At the same time there was all the political strife, the work of the new Constituent Assembly, and all the other social work going on. Economically we were focused on improving the price of oil; in the short term, this was the only way to increase our revenue.

But 600,000 children turned up for school; double what we had predicted. It was a crisis, but a beautiful crisis, because we were fighting to educate our children. We had to employ new teachers, pay lower salaries than usual, sign wage agreements, and invite retired teachers to give classes for free. Even soldiers gave classes. Some schools told kids, "You can't come if you don't have any shoes." I asked, "Why are shoes so important? If they had insisted that I wore shoes when I was a kid, I would never have made sixth grade." I used to go to school in homemade sandals, and when those broke, I went barefoot. At high school in Barinas, I used to wear rubber boots, and my clothes were usually tattered and torn. Why should we now demand that the kids wear shoes? Let them go barefoot, let them go in shorts. If they don't have any uniforms let them go in whatever they do have.

So in the social sphere we doubled the budget for health and education.

Then the tragedy in Vargas struck.[19] An avalanche devastated the entire state, bringing with it other, much more serious difficulties. There was a nationwide response of greater solidarity than ever before, and even middle-class and wealthy people helped by donating medicines. The whole world helped us. Cuba was the first to come forward, but the United States also sent helicopters. In the desolate streets of Vargas, so full of mud they looked like they'd been hit by an atomic bomb, there were doctors and paramedics from Cuba, France, Brazil, and Venezuela.

The tragedy increased our difficulties, but at the same time fortified our determination to overcome all obstacles. We recalled Bolívar's famous phrase uttered in 1812, during a terrible earthquake in Caracas. Priests and prophets were claiming the disaster was divine punishment for the declaration of independence and the war against the king. Simón Bolívar said, "If nature stands against us, we will fight her." We repeated this same phrase at that time. If nature opposes us we shall fight her as well.

In 1999 we implemented social programs and by 2000, with more resources for education and health, unemployment began to fall. In the middle of the 1999 crisis we set up the People's Bank, inspired by a Bangladeshi example where a noncommercial bank had been established not to make money but to grant micro-credits. We provided a very limited budget and the People's Bank began to give small loans. Bankers, financiers, and economists all laughed at us and said, "Look at crazy Chávez giving $100 loans!" Sometimes the loans were even less and many were granted without interest; disabled people for example were not charged interest. The People's Bank was born and began to grant micro-credits. We created a single fund combining all the old social welfare programs that were often useless centers of corruption and waste. We brought all these together into the single social welfare fund. In 1999 we also introduced some new laws in order to strengthen the social projects.

By 2000 we were entering a new period of economic stability. We went to elections again and were re-elected with a larger majority. We called these new elections because the Bolivarian constitution allowed for this option. Some said it wasn't necessary, but it was the decision of the Constituent Assembly, which I totally agreed with. The new constitution closed the door on the past and the assembly called general elections. I even put my position up for election. Mine, together with all the governors' posts — the majority of whom were against the revolution — and those of the congress, which is now the National Assembly. This enabled us to later change the Supreme Court and the National Electoral Council.

Elections were justified because a new era in the life of the nation had just begun.

My presidential term was cut short. I had been elected for five years but that government was in office for just two. I was then re-elected for six years, in accordance with the Bolivarian constitution. Governors were elected for four years and members of the National Assembly for five.

Returning to social issues: 2000 was a year of economic recovery in the midst of the oil crisis. Our intense international tours began to have some effect — foreign investment began to increase and we were able to dispel the neoliberal myth, which still exists in places, that the only way to attract international investment is by privatizing and granting favorable credit, basically selling the carpet from under your own feet.

We stopped the privatization of key industries, even of PDVSA [the national oil company] itself.[20] We traveled around the world, to Italy, France, Germany, Russia, China, and India, to explain our projects to presidents, royalty, and business people. Little by little this began to pay off. The French began to arrive. The US business that was already here didn't leave. We guaranteed oil companies' investments, providing they paid their taxes. They were worried when we changed the tax system, because previously they had paid very little tax and now they had to pay more.

We began to recover socially and economically and continued to create new institutions. By 2000 we had a National Assembly in place, where we had a more than two-thirds majority, although some people wanted to "have it all their own way," as we say here. People started to "climb on to the bandwagon" with ulterior motives. A group of political dealers — a political mafia — initially allied itself with us. They were policy traffickers, gold diggers, and treasure hunters, riddled with bad intentions. There were several reasons for this. A number of individuals lacked ideological consistency; others infiltrated the movement, giving pseudo-revolutionary speeches, Bolivarian in content but self-seeking in reality. Other groups or parties appeared, such as Movement Toward Socialism (MAS), which is not a movement at all and neither is it socialist in any way; it is only a group of political dealers and mafia. They aligned themselves to us and in this way became parliamentary delegates; later on there was a split in this party, with its veteran leaders joining the opposition.

At the same time Operation Siege was launched, which was a plan to fence me in. The oligarchy was heard to say, "If we can't kill the beast, we will tame it." I was the beast, and this wouldn't have been the first time. There have been other beasts here and they have all been tamed in the end. Páez is an example,[21] my General Páez, hero of the independence struggle, Lion of Queseras, invincible man of the Venezuelan plains, "foremost spear in the world," as Bolívar described him. Páez was tamed in the end, and used his spear at the behest of the oligarchy. He betrayed his people and died old and rich in New York. I believe he regretted his behavior: I once read his lengthy memoirs, and in the final few pages of one volume he says, "I, José Antonio Páez, born in Curpa, in the province of Barinas, Venezuela, of the line of liberators of Venezuela, would have preferred to die on the battlefield."

There are many other examples. We had a federal war here and it was Zamora,[22] my general, who demanded land for the peasant farmers, went to war, and his military commanders gained power. He was a great revolutionary who said, "land and free men…" Yet he ended up the same as all the others; like Guzmán Blanco, for example, who turned French, dying a wealthy man in Paris while the people remained poor, betrayed, and deceived. Guzmán Blanco won power with an old slogan: if you can't beat the enemy, join them. I was just a kid; he was 45 or 46 years old. I was naïve, very naïve. Politically speaking, pardon the expression, I was a virgin.

I have had to learn the hard way, by developing consciousness and by studying. Thanks to a lot of people we have managed to learn, although I cannot deny that I have been surrounded by *zamuros*.[23]

I remember Venevisión, a TV channel that was the spearhead of the coup d'état; well in the early days, I was practically king of Venevisión. As president-elect, they invited me to participate in a four-hour TV program. They even managed to find a photo of me when I was about two, together with my brother Adán, the only photo of me as a baby, naked and covering my private parts with a handkerchief. I was tiny and had hardly any hair. The program presenter, who these days is anti-Chavista through and through, commented, "How cute the president was, how cute he was." The whole scene was embarrassing, and it was a plan to lure me over to their side. Yet that little beast [in the photograph] turned out to be a hell of a beast, and little by little he cut them off. The majority [of those people] — rats[24] — were cornered in their own lair, their own trenches, which is where we have them today.

This is a key point I am making. Some writers, analysts, journalists, spread around the idea that Chávez had brought about a miracle: without making a revolution, he had caused a counterrevolution. What an odd thing to say. These are people with Marxist backgrounds who have surrendered to the enemy. In certain circles an entire thesis has been developed along these lines, particularly in Venezuela, but also in other countries. Yet, from a mathematical or a scientific point of view, this is impossible. There cannot be a reaction without a previous action. It is impossible for poppies to flower in the desert;

something has to happen first. Don't be misled, look under the sand, there has to be something beneath it: fertilizer. Someone supplied fertile soil and fertilizer so that plants might grow there.

The national oligarchy

It is clear that a revolutionary process, of a specifc character, is underway here. The question is whether the Venezuelan oligarchy — the
wealthy, in other words — have lost out because of it. I would say
that as individuals, they have not been targeted; no one has attacked
them. This is also the case with regard to family or small businesses;
none of these have been expropriated. At higher levels, however,
they have been affected, and quite markedly so. In the first place,
until February 2, 1999, we had a government here that was obedient
to orders from Washington; the government here was not Venezuelan.
Lackeys held power here for a long time.

This is an important element worth noting: this affected not only
what happened in Venezuela, but also internationally. For example,
Venezuela participated actively in the struggle against the Colombian guerrilla forces. I was in Colombia. I was second lieutenant —
before the Bolivarian army surfaced — pursuing Colombian guerrilla
fighters on border patrol. Later, as a captain, following instructions
from the military command whose orders I obeyed, we went by air to
Colombia to meet with members of the Colombian armed forces. I
attended a number of meetings with Colombian soldiers; the strategy
was to fight the common enemy, the Colombian guerrilla forces. I
remarked to my colleagues that when there were guerrillas in Venezuela, a decade previously, we had also been present when those
suspected guerrillas had been beaten up. I was opposed to the

beatings, but they were prisoners and I was a soldier. I also saw some soldiers massacred by Venezuelan guerrillas, one of them died in my arms. I will never forget the look in his eyes, "Lieutenant, don't let me die." He died. That was in 1977.

In the 1980s, we were mobilized and taken to the border to participate in the war, under Washington's orders. Since then there has been a major change at the international level. From the very first day [of our government's term] we refused, arguing that the war was Colombia's internal problem and that the role of the Venezuelan army was to preserve the sovereignty of Venezuela and prevent the conflict from spilling over. We told them not to request that we carry out joint military exercises. From Clinton to the different "misters" who turned up—generals, civilians, military personnel, Colombians—to Señor Pastrana and his generals,[25] we told them not to ask us to transport weapons through Venezuelan territory that would be used to surround the guerrilla forces on the other side. And in this sense we respected Colombia's sovereignty.

Generally speaking, relations with private companies have been poor, above all because the Venezuelan private sector has to a large extent been in decline over recent decades. Phony business people abound here, they are not real business people, they have virtually no assets or investments in the country, they have no payrolls or employees, they are simply briefcase-carrying people who became wealthy at the expense of the state. Thanks to such contracts and corruption, these people became an antinationalist elite. I mentioned this to Lula [da Silva],[26] who felt that the Brazilian business class was pro-nationalist, proud to be Brazilian, and was making an effort to strengthen Brazil. This is not the case in Venezuela, insofar as big business is concerned.

Economic interests are what count to capitalists—sovereignty is not an issue, neither are a few deaths, none of this is important. They care about how much is in their wallets and in their dollar bank accounts. What was happening in Venezuela was nothing less than the privatization of the country's oil industry. This project had been underway for at least five years. They had privatized part of the industry, of PDVSA. Since the 2002 coup we have reversed this process. They had gone so far as to privatize the brain of PDVSA, and were handing it over to a US company under CIA management. Just imagine what they were handing over!

PDVSA represents not only the assets Venezuela possesses today, which are sizable, but also the country's vast [unexploited] oil and gas reserves. If we add, as we should, the Orinoco oil belt, Venezuela has, or will have, one of the largest oil reserves in the world, even compared to the oil fields of the Persian Gulf. Our government brought that privatization to a complete halt, and not only stopped it, but also began a counteroffensive. We introduced the new hydrocarbons law, and it was established definitively in the Venezuelan constitution that the PDVSA will always belong to the state.

This series of measures affected the imperialists and key capitalist interests, above all the interests of transnationals that had their eyes on the oil here and had heavily invested in training, and buying, Venezuelan technicians. Technicians here had been brainwashed; they didn't obey the Venezuelan government, but a transnational government. This is the technocratic elite that rebelled against us in the oil strike. Venezuelans brought their own oil industry to a halt; they stopped ships and sabotaged refineries under orders from abroad. As far as we know, this has not been done anywhere else in the world. They had a plan and had been handing over the company and Venezuelan oil to big business. Just think about how far they went. It had worldwide repercussions. The April coup was a coup for oil, a coup that had the strong smell of oil.

In fact, there was a business lockout; supermarkets were shut down, as was the agricultural and manufacturing sector. These businesses closed their doors under pressure, as did other sectors such as retail and manufacturing. In spite of all of this, the nationalization of supermarkets, of shops, is not part of our plans. Large-scale agro businesses took it on themselves to deliberately sabotage meat production. They went so far as to boycott the supply of milk, even pouring it down the drains; they sent armed groups to damage the dairy production machinery and prevent the distribution of milk.

From the perspective of state participation in the economy, our plans are focused on PDVSA, which is most important. As someone said, PDVSA is a bull in a China shop. We brought the process of privatization to a halt, which was the key element in the sabotaging of oil and the economy, and in the political and economic battle.

We decided to set up state-owned companies instead of nationalizing private firms, and to occupy niche markets in order to compete with them. We established an agricultural company; in fact it already existed, but it comprised only an empty shell of buildings. The state had no experience in agriculture, not even in importing. We did not know how or where to buy a black bean. We did not have the facilities or the assets to store food in silos, and there was zero state distribution and transportation of food; all this was in private hands. Now, however, we are concentrating on organizing and creating state or public concerns that are responsible for the distribution of foodstuffs.

Regarding production, last night I signed a document authorizing the purchase of a sugar mill from private owners in the east of the country. We plan to form a state-owned company managed in partnership with the workers. This is a way to move progressively toward a mixed model of partnership between the state and, above all, cooperatives.

In the end, all this depends on our perspective, on what meaning we attribute to being more radical. The reality is that we were on the threshold of a situation that forced us, even though it wasn't part of our plan, to take measures regarding nationalization.

For example, take the banking sector, private banks. Banks backed the economic sabotage; they kept their branches closed so that people could not withdraw from their accounts. Banks were opened for an hour, from 11 to 12 noon. Lines of people waited in the sun, with no shade or protection, because of the banks, not because of any crisis. Many people had money held against their will by the banks and the bankers. So we gave the banks a deadline. It was January, and we summoned the bankers. We gave them a fixed date and said that if they continued to act in such a way we would take control of the banks within a week. We were prepared to do it. According to Venezuelan law intervention is permitted, first by declaring a financial or banking emergency, then the state takes control of the bank and appoints a board of directors. The next phase would be nationalization.

You must remember that we have inherited a series of laws. Given the pacific and democratic nature of our process, we have to operate within this framework, according to these laws. For example, a few months back we expropriated private, or supposedly private, land — land that had been abandoned. Some 10,000 hectares in the plains region belonged to individuals who said they were the owners of this land, even though it had been abandoned. We handed the land over to farmers; we gave them land deeds, and occupied the land. Four months later, at the start of this year, a court ruled that we had to return the land to the owners. It is a judicial mess: evidence now has to be provided of who has ownership rights, these individuals or the state. A year or two will be spent on this.

Something needs to be taken into account here: the difference between our court cases and others, such as those in Cuba, for example. We are obliged to respect laws that are very often contradictory to, or put the brakes on, the revolutionary process itself. That is a heavy burden for us to bear.

The Missions

In 1999 we were on the defensive, socially speaking. Some initiatives had been taken, but the avalanche, the real offensive, took place with Plan Bolívar in 2000. We invested more resources in Plan Bolívar and began a nationwide overhaul of the health system, starting with the repair of outpatient centers and hospital equipment, which throughout the country was practically useless. At that time two-thirds of local government councils were with us; this is the importance of the new mandate, we won over 15 local governments and almost 50 percent of the governors' offices, meaning that we now had a majority in government and an improved capacity to increase the effectiveness our social policies.

Then 2001 arrived; the year we went on the offensive, socially speaking, particularly with the empowerment law. This was the catalyst for the coup d'état. Until then the oligarchy had been flirting with us, negotiating or attempting to negotiate. But they realized we were serious about transforming the political and economic spheres. The empowerment law, a mechanism that has always existed in the old constitution and still exists in the new one, enabled us to halt the PDVSA privatizations and also the privatization of CVG and the entire aluminum industry.[27] The oligarchy reacted with anger.

The congress or National Assembly empowers the Council of Ministers president to pass laws, but within a framework previously defined by the assembly. These laws are debated again by assembly, which has the power to revise and modify them. The assembly granted legislative authority to the Council of Ministers and we began to pass laws, especially laws relating to the social sphere. We passed 49 laws in one year and almost all of them were profoundly social in content. The land law, for example, unleashed the fury of the oligarchy. There was a new banking law, and fishing legislation to confront the difficulties in the fishing industry. There was legislation regarding agriculture, hydrocarbons, and much more. We set about modifying old legislation, following a very clear philosophy: if we wanted to put an end to poverty, we should empower the poor.

This project of transformation means that, little by little, people who have been excluded will have access to posts and become empowered. This is true democracy, extending far beyond formal political democracy that limits choice to whether or not a particular governor should be elected.

The year 2001 was a year of social progress, structurally speaking as well. Of course, this infuriated the serpent in its totality: there was the business lockout of December 2001 and the conspiracy was set in motion, culminating in the coup d'état. The coup was very damaging for us; the social progress that was taking place and making an impact was brought to a standstill. Unemployment figures rose again and companies went bankrupt, particularly small- and medium-sized businesses. Housing projects, another of the major social initiatives, came to a halt. From 1999 until 2001, in spite of limited resources, we had constructed many houses.

On one occasion a man who had been granted a house said to me, "Chávez, now I have no reason to envy the rich because I have a fantastic, dignified home, a home just for me." We had made huge progress and then in 2002 it came to a complete stop. That was very hard for me to take. We are resuming work again, but the damage to the economy and, of course, to the social welfare programs, was serious.

Social welfare programs were brought to a standstill, there was increased unemployment, inflation, and capital flight; all of this resurged. We had already defeated inflation, and our international reserves were more than $21 billion. Almost all of it was stripped away, we had to apply extraordinary restrictions on currency exchange, and suffered another crisis, and so the social welfare missions were devised.

I remember during a conversation with Fidel I suggested the idea of a literacy campaign. The campaign was initially to take place on a small scale. Then, returning from the Ibero-American Summit in Santa Cruz de la Sierra in Bolivia, we put both our heads together, minds that are resourceful, very resourceful! Fidel had already begun to mobilize people in Cuba and I was calling on people here, because we had devised a little plan. A Cuban comrade related this story to me. When Fidel arrived back in Cuba, he called a meeting one night. He said, "Listen, this is the plan, how long will it take to carry out?" This was the plan for the family libraries.[28] "How long will it take us to print one million libraries?"

"What do you mean, a million? Wasn't it 100,000?"

"It's a million. How long?"

So then she answered, "Well, it will take six months, *comandante*."

"Six months, are you crazy?" was Fidel's reply.

She remarked to me, "He said I was crazy, but he's the one who is crazy, and you too. You are two mad men who have got the idea of this race into your heads." But it was accomplished, the libraries arrived, and one literacy mission after another emerged: Mission Robinson,[29] Mission Ribas.[30] And with Cuban support, there will be no end to this.

I explained this in Monterrey [at the Summit of the Americas]. President Bush's speech seemed contemptible to me, and even more contemptible was that everyone else kept their mouths shut about it. But practically everyone attacked Cuba in its absence. When it was my turn to talk I thanked Cuba. That year in Venezuela we managed to reduce inequality, and we did this thanks to Cuba and the efforts of Cubans and Venezuelans. These missions were born out of a joint effort and the cooperation agreement Fidel and I signed in 2001. Look at the outcomes up to now.

Historically, the annual figure for those reaching proficient literacy levels in Venezuela was 15,000, and that figure is above average. In six months of 2003 alone, we taught one million people to read and write. The rate skyrocketed from 15,000 to one million a year.

And it was done with quality, as the immortal Che used to say. We have quoted Che often on this matter, saying again and again, *no bojote*.[31] Che said that poor quality is at odds with the revolution. Everything must be done well. We have been very strict about that, carefully observing, assessing, and facilitating the process. For example, I have seen with my own eyes how a 102-year-old man, who had never been to school, learned to read and write in seven weeks, as did an 85-year-old woman. Siblings of 8, 10, and 12 years of age, whose father had been killed, said to me in tears, "We have never been to school Mr. President and now we have learned how to read." Now they go to school and are part of the normal education system. This was the initial idea for education, but afterwards, because the mind is infinite, the plan for Mission Sucre emerged.[32] We reflected on the success of the 1.5 million illiterates who registered in the literacy program, and then wondered what was possible for those students who had finished high school but had no access to university education? That is how Mission Sucre surfaced. When we convened it one Sunday, another avalanche took place; over 600,000 people, perhaps closer to a million people, turned up.

After that we wondered how many people had begun primary school and not completed sixth grade. We called on these people too, and yet another avalanche came, another million in round figures. Finally, we devised the missing link. During a conversation with

Fidel in the early hours of one morning I told him we lacked the missing link. He replied, "The missing link, Chávez?"

"Yes, the missing link, those who began secondary education and didn't finish it." We called on them and they numbered almost 700,000. As you can see, each of these groups of human beings has a mission assigned to them. Right now in Venezuela, 60 percent of the population is studying.

[Former US President] Carter was correct when he visited us recently and met with the leading neighborhood figures here in Caracas. He raised the hackles of the oligarchy by revealing something he had told me in private but repeated on TV at a press conference. "I have just had one of the most wonderful meetings I've ever had in my life, with leaders of the people," he said. At that neighborhood meeting one man told him that there were 200,000 people living in his neighborhood, and that until now he had never seen a doctor. He was referring to Mission Barrio Adentro,[33] involving Cuban doctors. For over 40 years, the 200,000 people living in his neighborhood had never had a doctor. When they were sick they went to hospital; some died waiting for attention, women gave birth on the floor, children died of asthma and diarrhea. Now they have doctors. You won't find a single person in that neighborhood who says they don't have swift access, within an hour, to a doctor. Furthermore, the doctor comes with medicines; they don't have to buy it.

Carter's comment reflects this. He also related that someone else had joked to him that his neighborhood used to get together often in each other's homes, to dance and drink a few beers, but that now they only do this on Sundays. Why? Because most days after 5 p.m. everyone is studying, young and old.

Everyone is studying, learning to read and write or studying for high school exams. All the missions have begun, all of them. Someone asked me, "Are you crazy? Are we going to start every mission in the same year?" They are all underway, with the massive participation of the people of course, and, I repeat, with fantastic Cuban support. I will never tire of acknowledging this, of highlighting it and expressing my gratitude in public, wherever I am and whoever I am with, in whatever world forum I happen to be addressing, regardless of how many faces burn with anger because I refer to Cuba in these terms.

So then, missions Barrio Adentro, Robinson, Sucre, Ribas, and just recently we have launched a mission that is going to be phenomenal, Mission Vuelvan Caras,[34] in honor of an independence battle characterized by "*Vuelvan Caras*," Páez's war cry. We are returning the meaning of *Vuelvan Caras* to its people; it is a mission about training for work.

All these missions spring from and are designed out of direct contact with the people. The people want these missions. This contact has no substitute. I enjoy being right in there with the masses, listening to them and reading the numerous letters written to me, but above all it is important to talk, to take someone by the hand, even though it is for only 30 seconds or a minute.

A few months back, in December, one woman in the east of the country told me, "Chávez, I am studying. I am going to finish high school, Chávez." She must have been about 35 years old. Her children were studying at high school; she studied with her children. She went on to say, "My children are studying, my husband is unemployed, I am unemployed. I have grandchildren who we have to look after. We have problems, sometimes we don't have enough food to eat." On the plane home I thought about that conversation and realized something needed to be done. We set up the scholarship system, seeking resources from PDVSA, because for the first time in Venezuela's history, PDVSA is truly in public hands. Thanks to the revolution, oil belongs to the people of Venezuela. We have recovered it and the hundreds of millions of dollars that were being stolen from us and deposited in secret foreign bank accounts or distributed among foundations and funds. Now this money is going to the poor. We drew up a scholarship plan, which is just about to meet its goal of 400,000 grants of $100 a month per person. We haven't yet met the target, but we are getting there. However, there are not enough funds [to grant scholarships to everyone], which was why Mission Vuelvan Caras was established. Now we are initiating vocational training.

If you are studying math, you will be using textbooks from Havana — that is where they are printed. Videos teaching Spanish and literature also come from Havana. It is important for the world to know what Havana is doing. Venezuelans, and some Cuban professors, facilitate the classes, but most important is the massive commitment of young people. However, you could be studying math, biology, English, or computer studies, but if you have children and grandchildren at home, as that woman mentioned to me, "What about food?" This is why we devised Mission Vuelvan Caras, because it provides an opportunity for vocational training.

In this way, you can perhaps train in a trade, say, to make clothes. We are organizing cooperatives. As a slogan I have said that every classroom should be a cooperative, a cooperative that should control assets.

I have hardly slept, spending the early hours of each morning looking over papers and calling people. Just this morning I was overjoyed because I discovered that some land — 200 hectares on the mountain slopes near Caracas, out toward Teques — belongs to the Industrial Bank, which is state-owned and has been for some time. The Industrial Bank received this as payment from a debtor who couldn't repay a loan. It is 200 hectares of good land, which has been abandoned for over 10 years and which could be planted. The bank put it up for sale but no one was interested in buying . We have devised a way of dealing with the legalities of the situation. The Industrial Bank will loan this land to Mission Vuelvan Caras, so that it can be put to use. Who will work this land? Unemployed people, and those who are studying in all the missions. We will carry out studies of the soil to see whether it is good or not.

Another example I can give you is in the state of Zulia, where PDVSA has a massive facility. This facility has a lot of adjacent unused land; almost 1,000 hectares that is ideal for growing yucca to produce starch, which we currently import. Imagine the absurdity: the very same oil company then uses this imported starch. The market is guaranteed; instead of importing starch, let's plant yucca (with the necessary machinery, which is not that sophisticated), providing work for the unemployed in Mission Robinson, to produce starch to sell to PDVSA.

Two more examples: around here in Guarenas, close to Caracas, we discovered a spinning mill—a linen factory—that has been in the hands of the Industrial Bank for over 10 years. The bank was handed the mill as a form of payment and the mill is closed. The machinery is inside, all in good condition, and there is only one man who is responsible for maintaining it. We have decided to open the mill; the Industrial Bank will loan it to Mission Vuelvan Caras so that it can begin to produce linen.

There is also an [unused] military training ground, where we practice parachuting. I know several pieces of land in different parts of the country, roughly 10,000 hectares, and only half of this is used for military exercises. We have to be on guard, we have to train the people to defend our country, but we also have plans to use the other half for cattle breeding, because right now we are importing cattle. We have been importing over 60 percent of the meat we consume. For god's sake, how is it possible, with so much land and so much water and so many unemployed people, that we have had to import black beans, which you [in Cuba] call *frijoles*, from Argentina and Uruguay, and shipload after shipload of bananas? We should be growing them here.

In other words, the idea is training and work for production. This year will be crucial in socioeconomic terms. We have announced the revolution within the revolution: the socioeconomic consolidation we have achieved until now. Mao Tse-tung once said this back in the 1960s, during the Great Leap Forward, and that is what I have said to the Venezuelan people and the armed forces and, first and foremost, to myself. You are right [Aleida], when you claim I have been too soft on a number of occasions over these past five years and I accept responsibility for this.[35]

I came close to death. I am telling you this not simply because you are who you are, but because I am being completely honest. During the coup, at midnight on April 12, [2002], they were going to execute me on the beach; the order was that at sunrise I was to be a corpse.

I carried a crucifix in my hand; I thought of Christ and of Che. I was surrounded by kids whose minds had been poisoned, soldiers and mercenaries, armed with machine guns. One of them came up behind me and I thought he was going to shoot me in the back, so I turned around and looked directly into his eyes and at that moment Che Guevara came to mind, there in the tiny school in the village of La Higuera. I told myself, "You are going to die like a man, standing up." Fortunately, that incident did not end with my death, on account of the military circumstances. At that point, a helicopter flew in. The waves of the sea were crashing loudly, a star was shining, and men had their weapons aimed at me. I was ready to die. But suddenly one of the young soldiers, one of those guarding me, rifle in hand, said, "If we kill the president, we'll all die; he is the president of Venezuela." Chaos broke out and that is when I turned the tables and took control saying, "Calm down, calm down, you are my men." I began to talk to them and managed to get their cooperation and take control. I said, "Listen, I am a prisoner, treat me as a prisoner, but take into consideration that I am the president."

So they took me away and we went to sleep, almost all of us, to rest a little. I said, "Tomorrow will be a new day, let's see what happens, but please stay calm, don't start killing each other here."

But returning to the social question, that's what we were talking about. This year has to be the great leap forward for us, a revolution within the revolution; that's what I have told myself. I cannot ask of others what I cannot do myself, but this is not just about me, this is a collective effort. Karl Marx said that history is made by leaders, but within the framework of the conditions that history imposes on them. The leader has a role to play, that's what Fidel is doing in Cuba. Cuba would not be the same without Fidel, even though I am sure Cuba would continue. But Fidel has played a crucial role — as did Che and Camilo[36] — Fidel and the masses. This is not the theory of the necessary caudillo; it is rather the Marxist or Marxian thesis that a leader makes history at the behest of history. A leader is partly a prisoner of history itself, of historical conditions.

It is clear that my willingness prior to April 11 to be flexible over and again gave rise to or allowed a number of events to unfold. In the first place, in terms of the armed forces, they were in the grip of the coup leaders. Now, for example, I could try to close down the TV channels [that backed the coup], even though I might fail in the attempt. But I have promised myself that if this opposition, this counterrevolution, this fascism, were to be unleashed again, I would not allow my country, our country, to be driven to the edge of the abyss, as it was on April 11.

There was a lesson for all of us, including me, in the people's response to the coup. When I was in prison after the crisis of that night had ended, when they were going to shoot me, I began moving little by little toward the offensive, ethically and mentally. I said to myself, "We will return, we will be back." I figured that it would take between several months and one or two years, but in the end I was back in the palace in a few days. It was a miracle; the reaction of a people who took to the streets in their millions brought it about, as did the soldiers, who did not aim their weapons at anyone. On the contrary, they raised the flag and demanded a return to the constitution.

Going back to this year, we have Mission Vuelvan Caras, the consolidation of Barrio Adentro, Mission Mercal,[37] and the supply of food to the most vulnerable sectors. We are going to provide a 100 percent food subsidy to over half a million people in the most vulnerable sector. To those not quite so vulnerable, we are going to sell food at 50 percent of Mission Mercal prices, which are already below domestic market prices.

This year we are going to consolidate and intensify our efforts not just in economics but also undoubtedly in politics and in the social welfare sphere. There are plans for the Recall Referendum.[38] I am almost certain that it won't go ahead, even though we have to wait to hear what the arbiter's decision is, the umpire [the National Electoral Council], whether it is in, or strike. All the signs indicate [the latter], including the opposition's desperate declarations, announcing rebellions — they are like children playing baseball.

They remind me of my brother Adeliz. When he was five, my brother used to get very upset when we played baseball in the street. If we didn't let him play, he would cry; our mother would come out and threaten to put an end to the game. We were forced to let him play and even worse, he had to bat first, but he couldn't hit the ball. I would stand there with the rubber ball, he had his wooden plank, and I would throw the ball so he couldn't help but hit it and run. He would reach first base, and that's where we would trick him. We would tell him, stay there, you've reached first base, and the game would continue with him just standing there. But after a while he would realize what was going on and start crying again because he wanted to bat. The opposition is a little like this. If the arbiter says there won't be a referendum, "We'll rebel!" they say. It is out of despair; they might try to stir things up, but we won't allow them to, and at any rate they will not have the forces required to see it through.

Elections for governors and mayors will be held and I am convinced that we will have a resounding victory.[39] The economy will improve this year. The price of oil is fair. Our international reserves are above $22 billion; we are controlling the exchange rate, industry, and tourism. We also have comprehensive agricultural plans. The signs of growth are visible in the economy and in the social and political spheres, as well as at an international level. And luck is on our side. The United States no longer has the same power it had four years ago, when the Venezuelan government and myself, speaking on behalf of Venezuela, was all alone at the international summits that Fidel did not attend. I was alone, for example, at the Summit of the Americas. But now we have Lula in Brazil, further south there is Kirchner, in Argentina, and the winds of change are blowing strongly in Peru, Bolivia, Ecuador, Uruguay, and El Salvador; in other words, what Fidel prophesied. When I was in prison I read Tomás Borge's book *Face to Face with Fidel Castro*, an interview with Fidel, who claimed that there would be a new wave of change in Latin America, but in another century.[40] Well that wave has arrived. The change is here with us now.

Economic relations with Cuba

Fidel has been very consistent and very straight with us from the beginning. We have an exchange agreement. The logic of the agreement, from the point of view of economic exchange between two countries, is as follows: all those books printed in Cuba, for example, the paper, ink, labor, transportation, cost money. Logically, these expenses would be deducted from the debt Cuba has with Venezuela as a consequence of the oil agreement. This is the case not only with Cuba, but also with the Dominican Republic and Jamaica.

The many medicines supplied by Cuba for Mission Barrio Adentro cost money. But Fidel is generous and said to me early on, "Chávez, this medicine is not included in the exchange of goods and services." Other things are included, more structural things for example, such as equipment to increase the power and efficiency of the refineries. But all these plans, these missions, all this Cuban support, is not just being paid for with oil; we are [also] selling oil to Cuba and Cuba is paying us at the international rate. The mechanism of cooperation, known as the Caracas Agreement, establishes that we sell at a discount to our neighboring Latin American and Caribbean countries. These countries pay off the debt in the long term, at an interest rate of two percent, with a period of grace. Debt may also be paid, if there is agreement between the parties, with goods and services.

Cuba pays, and will pay down to the last cent, as we have explained, for the oil we are selling to them, like other neighboring countries. The only difference is that before, Venezuela didn't sell oil to Cuba. Why not? Because of a ruling from Washington, because of the blockade, and the Helms-Burton Law. We don't give a damn about this, Cuba is our sister country and we will sell to Cuba. Besides, this is a matter of business, and we are interested in doing business, in selling oil and gas.

On conclusion of this first part of the interview I gave Chávez, on behalf of the Che Guevara Studies Center and Ocean Press, books that are part of the Che Guevara Publishing Project. Chávez then invited us to take part in the TV program "Aló Presidente," due to be broadcast the following Sunday from Maracaibo.

The dialogue that took place during this TV program is published as an appendix to this book (see appendix 1). What Chávez said spontaneously about Che is very thought provoking.

Part Two: Reflections

Introduction

On the afternoon of Tuesday, February 10, we returned to the presidential residence to conduct the second and last part of the interview. On arrival we discovered that Chávez had just had a similar meeting. I thought that it would be tiring to subject him again to another batch of identical or very similar questions. Fortunately, this time we had decided to conduct the interview off-camera, thinking that perhaps this would facilitate a more relaxed discussion. We hadn't foreseen that he had another commitment following our conversation. According to my calculations, I needed at least two more hours and he could only give us one.

Nevertheless, a promise is a promise, and in spite of his look of resignation when I argued about the commitment he had made, the president lived up to his courteous reputation. By that time in the afternoon he had not yet eaten lunch, which is why we stopped the interview so that he could finish his meal.

We began the conversation with a brief reference to my interview with General Jorge García Carneiro, current Venezuelan minister of defense and head of the armed forces. Carneiro had spoken to us about his experiences in the April 2002 coup d'état and the role of the armed forces in social welfare work (see appendix 2). Chávez pursued this matter, describing those times and others like them, which was particularly interesting. No doubt, there were many areas left unexplored, but I hope the account that follows will help provide a better insight into this man who at this very moment is making history in the Americas.

The minister of defense and the coup d'état

The army in this country has traditionally made money out of buying out-of-date munitions. On one occasion they purchased multiple missile launchers from Israel which hit their targets but made no impact; it was as if the missiles were made of cardboard, they were harmless. There were mortars that never exploded, second-hand tanks that were wrecks after only a few years' use. In the Tiuna fort there is a vehicle cemetery, line upon line of trucks like a vast army of god-knows-how-many divisions, as if they had come from a war. Wrecks of vehicles that fell apart soon after being bought. There are well-known cases, such as the Yugoslav munitions and the MX30 tanks, renowned for their worthlessness and waste.

The top brass traditionally went so far as to choose their own replacement military officials; it was a kind of hereditary succession, involving deeply rooted corruption.

The revolution put an end to all of this. When I won the elections, Jorge García Carneiro was brigadier general, recently promoted, but the top brass had not included him among their chosen few. I decided to summon the top brass one by one, and send them to the border for a time. I appointed Carneiro as chief of the military residence and he was with me for a year in Miraflores Palace. From there he was promoted to major general and I sent him to the division here in Caracas. That's where he was when the coup d'état took place. No doubt he told you about it.

The coup was a time of great suffering. I learned about Fidel's concern when he spoke to my daughter, María Gabriela, and later on when he talked to Carneiro himself, to García Montoya,[1] and to Baduel.[2]

Carneiro was here and assumed his responsibilities very bravely. I spoke to him by phone a few times, by radio, and finally I said to him that he shouldn't be a martyr, that he should surrender. They had him surrounded but he was holding out. At that point they threatened to force me to resign and I told Carneiro that I knew he was in the fortress together with another battalion commander. The coup plotters had already begun internal military raids; they imprisoned Carneiro in a bathroom but he escaped. It was quite an odyssey! He went out and addressed the people. He got up on a tank with a megaphone in hand. These images will go down in history.

We saw the coup d'état coming, but because of the disinformation and the lack of accurate detection apparatus, we were not able to discover when, how, and where it was coming from. You could feel it in the air, even though I believed in and trusted the top military ranks, in the rank and file, and in García Carneiro, who was a general then, but who had subordinates and brigade commanders to deal with. I trusted the top ranks; I never suspected that some of them would back the coup. Events took place on different levels; evidently we did not have the appropriate means of preventing them, halting them.

Family memories

I was born on July 28, 1954. My mother was hoping for a girl and, as the good Catholic and Christian woman she is, she named her first boy Adán. I was going to be Eva to complete the paradise. I am her second son and therefore couldn't be called Eva. I was given my father's name, and my second name, Rafael, belongs to my maternal grandfather, Rafael Infante. When all is said and done, it was my mother who gave me my name; it is always like that in the end.

There is a total of six children in our family. Adán is the eldest; he is a communist. He was part of the group of students from the University of the Andes, in Mérida, as was Rafael Ramírez, the current minister for oil. These students were recruited by Douglas Bravo, who became a legend. I knew him well then, I still know him well. Sadly, he drifted away from us, but I worked with Douglas over a number of years on different projects. I met Douglas through my brother Adán, when I returned from the antiguerrilla camps, where as I told you torture and murder took place. I felt really out of place, at least in that part of the army. I clashed constantly with my superiors; I was arrested on a number of occasions, and I was often disciplined because I answered back and argued with them. "You behave like a lawyer," a captain once told me. I wanted to leave and study, and one weekend I went to Mérida and asked Adán to get me a place; by then he was a lecturer at the university. He had graduated in physics and continued in the same university giving classes.

That was back in 1977 and at that time, I still felt young and that I had taken the wrong route, that I didn't want to be a soldier any longer. I had no idea about the movements Adán was involved in, which were still operating clandestinely. Douglas Bravo had not yet opted for peaceful means, he was still underground and moving around clandestinely. That was the time of the split in the Venezuelan Revolution Party (PRV). The PRV was a semi-clandestine party, whose members were persecuted. Some of its people were armed and operating in the mountains, small groups that had been militarily defeated, but were looking for a political path. They infiltrated the universities in search of young people.

Adán joined these groups and so did Rafael Ramírez and Tárek, a parliamentary representative currently running for governor; they all belonged to the PRV youth. When I asked Adán to get me into a course at the university, he replied immediately that I was crazy. He questioned how I would ask for permission to resign and said that I had to remain in the army. Then he told me what he was involved in. He explained that he was in the PRV with Douglas Bravo, who included work with active military forces among his plans. Some soldiers, very few, had joined him; they were mainly retired from the army and were collaborating with him to some degree, but he had practically nobody in the garrisons. A doctor had joined them, he wasn't a professional soldier but worked in the air force. Commander Izarra had joined as well,[3] but he was abroad.

After a few weeks I met Douglas Bravo. He inspired me and I realized I wouldn't be leaving the army. I discovered ideological meaning in civil-military work and possibilities for underground work, a phase that lasted several years. From 1978 to 1982, for almost five years, I had contact with Douglas. Later we drifted apart because he had his sights set on becoming a kind of caudillo, something I frequently argued with him about. In addition to other issues, he viewed professional soldiers as if we were [only] the armed wing of the revolution.

From that time onward I regarded our project as a civil-military union. I did not agree that we should be perceived simply as an armed wing. Besides this debate, which was not even the main one, I proposed the active participation of the armed forces in the drafting of the political manifesto. I didn't want to attend meetings where the only subject was the number of officers we had with us and what the military plan was; I was interested in the political plan.

In this way I developed awareness. I began to sound out possible comrades: the first was a very close friend of mine, an officer who was like a brother, and who knew about my initial involvement in the plot. One day, during a conversation that was not about politics, it crossed my mind to tell him we were going to talk to Douglas Bravo. He reacted by calling me crazy and saying that the guy was a communist, a guerrilla who killed soldiers. I immediately replied that this was not the case, that this was a lie being spread about. After that I talked to another man whose memories of the years of guerrilla struggle were still vivid enough for him to have a negative picture of Douglas Bravo. However, I didn't swallow his version or those put forward by my closest friends; we argued, but they didn't understand.

So my relations with the movement were, above all, personal. I continued working but within a Bolivarian and national profile and I realized that this could indeed penetrate the armed forces, like a seed in fèrtile soil. On the other hand, if you talked about former guerrilla fighters, tension surfaced and it became very difficult to make progress, to have discussions; rejection was natural, above all because of their military training.

Returning to the subject of my family. I have mentioned Adán and myself. Narciso came next and he is in Havana; he is an agricultural expert and an English teacher. Aníbal is a history graduate and a lecturer; Argenis is an electronics engineer and Adeliz, an economist, is number six. One brother died when he was very young, he was called Enzo and he brought the number up to six; he was born after Argenis. He died when he was six months old of leukemia, or something similar.

My social background is of poor peasant stock. We were, you could say, from the lowest class. We were born in a house made of palm trees; the walls were made of clay mixed with straw, wattle and daub. We owned nothing. Papá was a schoolmaster but he himself had barely finished sixth grade. He became a teacher by attending courses and over the years he earned his teaching diploma. Mamá was the same; she's from a very poor peasant family who owned no property, in Rastrojo, a remote area of the countryside.

Family relationships were very close in the early years, particularly with my grandmother on my father's side, because she brought us up. My grandmother Rosa Inés reared me. My mother used to tell me that when she gave birth to Adán, the eldest, she went to the village where the midwife was. There were no midwives and no electricity generators in the mountainous region where they lived — there was nothing — so my father took my mother to his mother, my grandmother Rosa's house in the village, to give birth.

My mother spent some time there with the baby, and then she returned home. I am not sure why Adán stayed in our grandmother's house, I have never asked her. The fact is that our mother returned home with our father and Adán remained; the same happened with me. I too stayed with our grandmother, in a house made out of palms. Obviously, we were always close by to our parents; we saw each other at weekends when they traveled into the village by bicycle. Then Narciso was born and my parents moved to the village. My father built a little house diagonally opposite my grandmother's house. My mother and father lived there with the other children; it was a little brick house with an asbestos roof and a cement floor. So they were less than 50 meters away from Adán, my grandmother, and myself.

I knew nothing about my grandfather; he was never mentioned, my grandmother never spoke about him. Less than a week ago my father visited and we had lunch together. I used the opportunity to ask him my grandfather's name.

My grandmother had two children, Marcos Chávez and Hugo, my father, by different men. Marcos is white; my grandmother once told me that Marcos's father was Italian and his surname was Binonio, or something like that. As far as my father's father is concerned… when I recently asked my father, he told me, almost 50 years on, that his name was Jorge Rafael Saavedra and that he was a *coleador*, the man who releases the bull into the arena that is chased by men on horseback who bring it down with their lassoes.

I asked my father if he had known my grandfather and he said "no." When he was very little, his father had gone to Guanarito, a nearby village, and married there. He had two other children; one of them is called Rafael and is a *coleador* just like his father. He only saw him once, when he got sick and asked to see him. Otherwise his mother wouldn't allow it. So it is only now, 50 years later, that I have an idea of who my paternal grandfather was: a *coleador*. He left and never came back, he had another family, a wife and other children, in Guanare, in the plains region.

On the other hand, my grandmother, La Rosa, was the best in the world. She was full of love and she was also like a teacher to us. She taught me to read, to work, to be honorable.

I remember that she taught us to read with a magazine called *Tricolor*. I will never forget the night I said to her, "Mamá Rosa" (we didn't call her granny, Mamá Elena was my mother, but there was Mamá Rosa too), "It says *rolo* here."

"Son, where does it say *rolo*?" She had a way of putting things.

"It says *rolo* here," I replied. The word was *tricolor* and I was reading it in reverse. I insisted I was right, saying, "Don't you see, it says *rolo, rolo*." She said, "Hey! This boy reads from there to here!"

She called me a "rearranger," and said that I rearranged things a lot. I remember a lot about her. I learned how to work thanks to my grandmother. When the rainy season came, the corn had to be sown, yards had to be cleaned, and later the corn had to be harvested and ground. Those years, from when I was about 8 to 12, were years of hard work with her. Poverty forced us to be resourceful. My grandmother was a hardworking woman who did everything: she made coconut buns and papaya cakes, which we called "spiders" because the fruit had to be cut up finely. They used to call me "spider boy" because I sold little bags of papaya cakes. Adán helped too, but less than me; he was a bit work shy. Me, I liked it. When she told me to look for the papaya I knew it was time to look for unripe, green papayas, peel them, open them, throw away the seeds, chop them up finely, cook them and add sugar and then the spiders were ready. Then we would set about selling them; we had to sell them. She would give me 10 spiders in a bag. I would head for school and sit at my desk with my bag beneath it. When the half-hour or 20-minute break came I would go out to sell the spiders for a *locha*, which was an eighth of a bolívar.

Oh! She wanted the accounts from me when I arrived home from school saying, "Here I am granny; I've sold them all." I nearly always sold all of them — there were some kids in my class who were quite well off and always had a *locha* to pay for a snack. I had my regular customers.

There was a pretty girl called Luz Colmenares, no, Contreras. Luz was the daughter of the richest people in the village and she always bought two spiders from me every day. So I was always certain to sell two spiders. She used to ask me to put them to one side for her because she really liked them, and the other kids did too. Sometimes the teachers would buy from me — they were really tasty and nobody else in the village made them.

All this took place in the south, in Sabaneta, Barinas, in the plains region. If I took 10 spiders to sell, I had to give 10 *lochas* to my grandmother, and she would give me back one. I had a little plastic piggy bank and I put them in there. From time to time, when I was a bit older, I would take a larger pot filled with spiders to sell at the alley, where people played *bolo*. *Bolo*, not *bulí*, which you [in Cuba] call bowling, is a game played on a smooth surface, in a long hall, where three skittles are placed at the far end and a wooden ball is aimed at them. Wham! The ball knocks them down, like nine pin, but rural style, from the plains. I used to go there to sell the spiders and to the cockfights or to the festivals held in honor of the village patron saint, Our Lady of the Rosary, on October 7. I used to sell up to three pots of spiders a day, which was quite a bit of money, and we used it to buy food, canvas shoes, my notebooks. My grandmother had an industry going, a small business, and I was part of this small business. Producer and seller.

As you can see, I learned a lot from my grandmother. I always liked the work, working the land, the nice work with the fruit, and selling things. My grandmother was very generous. She always said, "Hugo, Huguito, go to the *barquillería*," as she called the ice cream parlor, because you had to eat ice cream off the wafers (*barquilla*). We used to sell oranges to the *barquillería*, a sack of oranges used for making juice, sweets, and ice cream. We would sell 500 oranges for 5 bolívars. I always used a wheelbarrow — I was never afraid of work, I got used to it. I would climb an orange tree with my brother Nacho, who most liked to work with me. Not Adán, he was more intellectual; he helped, but not much, he was a bit slack as far as work was concerned. Nacho helped: we would climb the tree, or I would go up and throw oranges down to him one by one so they didn't split. That way he would fill the sack up. Then we would have to take them in the wheelbarrow. My grandmother always used to say to me, "Fill it with 120 oranges, give the extras away to the owners of the *barquillería*," who were Italian.

We sold avocados as well as papaya; there was an avocado tree, we loaded them up and sold them. My grandmother also made a dessert filled with fruit that she would give away, "Take a dish to Doña María." My grandmother taught me a lot: I learned to read and write, I learned to cherish the little birds and to water the plants.

I was not a difficult child, at least not with my grandmother. I was with my mother though, I don't know why. Once she was going to hit me and I actually grabbed the stick from her and ran away into the mountains. I was also uncooperative when it came to doctors. I was both a coward and a rebel. Being cowardly made me a rebel, and my reaction was to hide in the mountains. I climbed the tallest trees and hid. Once at vaccination time my father and some others had to bring me down, and hold me in order to vaccinate me. Imagine the scene, the four of them holding me down.

But, in fact, I did everything my grandmother asked me to do. She would say, "Huguito, go and water the plants," and I would take the little hose and water them. She also used to say, "Sing to the plants so they bloom more beautifully." People speak to them too — they say it's true — my grandmother and I sang to them. I watered and sang to them. I was happy. That was my grandmother. My grandmother was a treasure.

I always enjoyed singing; people called me the singer. One man, a singing teacher who came to the house from time to time, used to ask after the singer. I used to sing *rancheras*.[4] The music I like now is *llaneras*,[5] Venezuelan and Mexican music.

There was a song about a man with a sense of justice, called Rayo Rosales, "They called me Rayo / my Christian name is Mauricio Rosales." At the end he tells people to "respect the law." The guy was not very rebellious, "Live in peace, I am not saying good-bye or farewell because I am going and I am coming back." All the songs from Mexican cinema were very popular in the villages. We saw "Chucho el roto y los cinco halcones" at our village cinema, and we listened to Venezuelan music, our *llaneras,* which I loved, just as I loved Eneas Perdomo and Augusto Vargas, singers from those villages.

My grandmother was half-indigenous. She didn't sing, she was quite reserved, but she did talk to us, tell us stories. She was quiet-natured; I never saw her angry or out of control. She was calm, and always at peace with herself. She had beautiful long black hair and she was full of love. One night she told us about General Zamora and the five-year [Federal] War. She described how he and his men had passed by our village and when we asked, "Did you see them, Granny?" she replied, "No, my Mamá told me about it." My grandmother was right when she said that they had passed by to the sound of cornets and horses; in books I read later I came across the date when Zamora and the federal troops passed through that exact street. She told us her mother assured her they were heading for the Sabaneta hills, and that is what history records. In General Zamora's campaign diary, which I found later on, it is confirmed that on March 28, 1859, they passed by, just as my grandmother had said.

Besides Zamora, there was a lot of talk about a Chávez who had gone in search of Zamora and never returned. He went to join the war; I found that out later when I got the lists of Zamora's army, with the names of several Chávezes that were with him.

Some on my mother's side of the family said that I had a great grandfather who was a murderer. He was my mother's grandfather, Rafael Infante's father. But these are other grandmothers' stories. As you can see, it was all grandmothers and a lot of aunts; I never knew my grandfathers.

My mother's family was large and almost all of them were women. They were very pretty — we call them *catiras,* you call them blonds. My mother is a *catira,* her hair is the same color as yours; she is white and blond. My grandfather was also blond. Once we heard about the time our grandmother Martha scolded our mother. It was in Rastrojo one weekend, we had gone to see our grandmother and to eat papaya and play. My mother says that when she was young, less than 30 years old, my grandmother always scolded her for bad behavior. She was very strong willed. She said to her, "Elena, you are like that because you are an offshoot of that murderer; yes, that murderer, your grandfather, Rafael's father; he was a murderer. He killed a man called Bolívar; he tied him to a tree and shot him, and he cut off another man's head right in front of his children."

That is how I found out about my grandfather "the murderer." This story always disturbed me and over the years I searched for information about him. I discovered that he is in fact a legend; his legacy still haunts the paths he traveled. I learned that he was not a murderer, but a guerrilla fighter. When my grandfather Rafael and his brother Pedro were little—just like you, Aleida, when your father left—their father rebelled against the government. That was how I found out the truth and it freed me; I was finally able to tell my mother, when I was an officer in the army, that my grandfather was not a murderer.

I said to my mother that I had discovered the truth, or rather part of the truth, in a book. A book was published called *El último hombre a caballo* (The Last Man on Horseback). It is legendary. There was a poem as well, written by Andrés Eloy Blanco, one of the most important Venezuelan poets of the 19th century. He wrote a poem to my great grandfather, whom he met when he was taken prisoner on his journeys through the plains:

> Some call him Maisanta and others the American,
> But "American" is a lie because that blond boy is good.
> Between a bay and a chestnut he left Chiricoa
> With 40 men on horseback.
> There goes Pedro Pérez Delgado, heading for Menoveño
> In single file, across the dark savanna
> Rocking the cold in the old hammock
> To the revolutionary guerrilla war he goes.

With a *guama* hair blanket wrapped around his shoulders,
His .45 and cartridge belt, tobacco smoke and clouds,
A whinny and the cry of a heron,
Milky dawn beneath the icy night.

He was a guerrilla fighter, that's the truth. Perhaps because I didn't
know either of my grandfathers, and suddenly I got one, I was driven
to find out what he was and I went after him. I sought him in elderly
eyes and wrinkled faces.

Once, while I was still in the army, I traveled to Colombia looking
for him and was taken prisoner for it. I crossed the border without
authorization and I was carrying a regulation pistol. I was captured
by the Colombian army and accused of being a spy. For three days I
was imprisoned in Arauca, a military base. I was traveling around
interviewing elderly people. I was seized with, I don't know, a crav-
ing to know. I wanted to find out more, much more; I wanted to write
a book about my grandfather and his life, which spanned the end of
the 19th century and the start of the 20th. All that effort has contribu-
ted a lot to who I am today. I gathered the truth, I found explanations.

Broadly speaking, I have studied a lot. First there were the military
studies that, from 1971 onward, were graded at university level.
From that particular year you will find Jorge García Carneiro and
others of the first generation of university graduates in the military
academy. When I became a major I worked in Miraflores Palace, in
front of the White Palace; that was when I started a masters in political
science at the Simón Bolívar University. I was already involved in
the conspiracy and in order to find more theoretical tools, I studied.
I mostly studied in the afternoons. I left the White Palace at 4 p.m.,
the university was further away. I had classes from Mondays to
Thursdays; I finished all the coursework but I couldn't write the
thesis because the rebellion broke out. I was compiling information
for a thesis focused on the transition, or rather the model of a

transition, to a different situation; that was the thesis I wanted to write but was unable to.

I was authorized to continue working on this thesis in prison; I sent a letter to the university asking to be registered as a research student. It was very messy — I had to get lawyers involved, defending the prisoner's right to education — until in the end the minister of defense even authorized me to name my supervisor. I designated Jorge Giordani as my supervisor, current minister of planning. I have learned a lot from him throughout my life. Every Thursday Jorge came to Yare prison and we worked to fulfill all the requirements of a thesis, starting with the formulation of the question.

Then there was the second military rebellion,[6] on November 27 of the same year, 1992. After that, the prison was raided and they took away all our books, papers, everything. After this second rebellion it was prohibited to even have pencils in prison and, of course, Giordani was barred from entering. When I left prison we met up again and tried to resume work on the idea. But then there were the tours throughout the country, the public rallies, and it was practically impossible. We reached the conclusion that both the thesis and the problem were well defined, and that the idea of the transition was correct, but that it was not the time to write anything, instead we had to put the ideas into practice and bring about a transition.

In that period of my life, prison was not really what it was supposed to be; instead it was a school where I saw and learned from personal dynamics. It wasn't easy to be a prisoner moving within the dynamic of the different groups. I read in some book or other about the so-called madness of inmates, that is, when a prisoner reaches the point where for the simplest of reasons he fights with other inmates: because a plate falls to the floor or because you say something to me or because I think you said something or because you think who knows what about me. We experienced all the human misery there — we came into direct contact with it. You can see how envy takes hold of a group of comrades and how the enemy, the government and intelligence services of the day, know how to exploit that, to the extent that envy turns into hatred in some cases. In some cases it turned into attacks against me. Some said that I considered myself to be superior, that I thought I was a legend. Some said I was a legend, a hero, but I always challenged that idea. These are minor things but they influence people; you may not think so, but that's the way I saw it.

When visitors came to the prison, the majority of them came to my cell so that I could sign things, or they had their photo taken with me using hidden cameras ; that weighed on some people. Differences in political visions began to emerge: some proposed reform; others said there had to be a second military uprising because only certain forces had taken part [in the first]; some wanted to get out of jail as quickly as possible; some even sold information or negotiated with the government.

But in the end, those of us who confronted life in prison consciously, with dignity and integrity, left it strengthened. That is the severity of prison; that is why I deeply admire the five Cubans who are imprisoned in the United States.[7] The conditions they face are very harsh. I met Olga, René's wife, who came with her younger daughter and spoke at a public event we organized.

But, as I said, life also has its beautiful side. I like music, *rancheras*, romantic music, and I like to sing, I really enjoy singing. I imagine I am a singer, I love it. It is liberating to sing songs, like those of Alí Primera that I like a lot. I have all of his records.

Of course I like revolutionary songs too. I especially like the songs Alí Primera wrote for Che, like the song that goes like this:

> *Comandante* Che, they killed you
> but they left your memory
> in us forever

molded into casts of glory.
Through mountains and valleys
your memory wanders forever
your blood runs through our veins
swells in Bolivian chests.
Comandante Che, they killed you
but they left your memory
in us forever
molded into casts of glory.

And it ends like this:

When the current of the great Paraná
has no water left
then, perhaps then
comandante, amigo
you, you will leave us.

What a beautiful song!

When I was a lieutenant, being rebellious, I had a little device,
one of those portable things you can play cassettes on and I played
this music for the soldiers; imagine that, I was a second lieutenant!
A captain once called me crazy for playing music about Che Guevara
and Alí Primera in a garrison. But that's how we planted the seeds:
this music was a weapon for me, both here inside [he touches his
chest] and for the rest. Alí Primera harvested the people's feelings
and made them into a song.

I haven't listened that much to Víctor Jara; I know that he was killed when Allende was overthrown and that they cut his hands off.
Alí Primera wrote a song about him too, it is called, "Canción para
los valientes" (Song for the Brave):

Sing Víctor
Sing to the people
He who rebels is called upon.
Song of Chilean bones
Open fire, open fire
Chileans open fire
Open fire, open fire, open fire
For America open fire.
Sing Víctor
Sing to the people
He who rebels is called upon.
Song of Chilean bones
From deep within, song for the brave
that Víctor Jara sings
For comrade Allende.

And Neruda speaks:

Pablo Neruda does not sing
The general's verses.
He is too much of a poet
To see his people die
And survive it.

And he did go with the people; Neruda died shortly after the coup.

Military dictatorships in Latin America

The subject of the role of the armed forces and militarism in Latin America is very interesting. There have been major absences, weaknesses, and vacuums in the role of the military, even though in recent times there has been progress. The absences are being filled, strengthened. There is a logic behind this, not only at a national level, but at an international level.

There is the history of what happened with Pinochet and Víctor Jara; the sinister, terrible history of military coups and dictatorships in Latin America. I feel certain that this background, this cliché, has generated theoretical approaches regarding Venezuela that have caused confusion. In addition, the mass media took it upon themselves to spread this confusion about us, the armed forces, to hammer this confusion home in intellectual circles, both in Venezuela and in Latin America.

False documents were published in newspapers here in Venezuela, and radio and TV gave coverage to them. One paper published a list of so-called "executionable" personalities that included a group of intellectuals, with the outright intention of creating a consensus of opinion about me, before I even gained power. Our movement was defined in advance as militaristic, ultra-nationalistic, against independent thinking, and very similar, according to this false version, to the "*caras pintadas.*"[8] We were defenseless against the image of the dictator Pinochet, with his dark sunglasses and his horrible hat.

How could we defend ourselves against such an image? With cannons? This was artillery, heavy-duty artillery, and we were defenseless. We had no access to the daily newspapers, TV, or any other media. Not only the national press came down on us, the full weight of the international press came down too, imperialism's press.

While I was in prison, the Buenos Aires newspaper *El Clarín* published an article on "the Venezuelan *caras pintadas.*" We were forced to write a letter requesting the right of reply; I don't know if they ever published it, I don't think so. That was published in Uruguay and Paraguay and spread throughout the world. In the Southern Cone the military dictatorships were more ruthless, probably the most ruthless in world history. A few months after leaving prison we were invited to Buenos Aires and at that time the front-page headlines of all the newspapers declared, "The Venezuelan *cara pintada* has arrived." From that point on, left-wing movements in South and Central America began to view Chávez as a budding dictator, a right-winger.

On one occasion I was invited to the Sao Paolo Forum in San Salvador.[9] Shafik Handal invited me at Cuba's request. I went with a comrade, we didn't have the money for the ticket but we went anyway. Many people there began to argue about my presence and I was not allowed to speak, to give my greetings, at the plenary session. Shafik had to take me to one side and apologize. He was very embarrassed, though I told him not to worry — I had not come to seek fame. I didn't know Shafik then, and I explained to him that I had come, because I had been invited, to participate as an observer, and that he shouldn't be concerned. However, in spite of opposition by some movements and left-wing parties from Mexico, Argentina, and the Caribbean, we took part in several round-table discussions.

At the same time, left-wing intellectuals are few and far between in these parts (and those who truly are left-wing must be very well-educated, because degeneracy has taken hold of many of them). In the 1970s and 1980s many of them sold out, often to the worst parties. We have in Venezuela the example of writer and journalist Teodoro Petkoff who was paid to write editorials. People like this damaged our position, for example in Colombia, where news was circulated that our movement was aligned with the Colombian guerrilla forces. Undoubtedly, this had negative repercussions for some sectors in Colombia, especially for those left-wing sectors that do not approve of the guerrilla methods, methods that are often hard to understand. Sometimes you can share ideas, intentions, philosophy, politics... but to bomb a church in which there are women and children, that is beyond the bounds of comprehension. Sometimes these guerrilla methods or the debates about them are difficult to understand, but that is another problem altogether.

In other words, I am looking for reasons for the vacuums in the armed forces, both here and in Latin America...

Intellectuals, at least in our societies, and even in left-wing societies, tend to live in middle-class or even upper middle-class neighborhoods. In Venezuela's political climate, a fascist method of intimidation has been employed, involving even physical attacks against individuals, often among neighbors. There are intellectuals who sympathize with our project, perhaps not in its entirety, but at least they have a positive attitude toward it. But they don't dare talk about this; they prefer to keep quiet because they are afraid of the pressure, this social blackmail, prevailing in their own environment.

After the April 11, 2002, coup d'état, currents of opinion have emerged, particularly at an international level, that are supportive of our process. I attended a forum in Paris organized in October 2001, which is where I met Ignacio Ramonet, Bernal Cáceres, the US writer James Petras, and others. I was amazed, the auditorium at the Sorbonne was full. Ignacio Ramonet improvised a speech putting forward a surprising analysis of Venezuela. I invited him to come here, which he did, one week before the coup. We went out together at midnight driving around Caracas. (I love going out at night, driving around the streets; I wanted to take you out but they wouldn't let me.)

One of Ramonet's remarks caused me to think. He said he had been observing the situation in Venezuela for a year or so and had also been receiving news from Latin America. He believed that the case of Venezuela was worth studying because Venezuela was developing in a manner that was outside the prevailing world model since the collapse of the Soviet Union and the Berlin Wall. Neoliberalism was proclaiming victory, like Tarzan. It advocated the end of history, the last man, and all these ideas. Throughout the entire world, with the exception of China and Cuba, and particularly in the western world, in North and South America and in Europe, neoliberalism was accepted as the definitive path. Russia had also begun to seek the route to the free market, which would have been unthinkable 20 years ago. Ramonet commented that within this framework Venezuela had behaved strangely right from the start, and that's true. The Caracazo took place here in 1989, when the Soviet debacle was beginning. It was then that Carlos Andrés Pérez attempted to apply the IMF recipe, the politics of shock therapy, and the people rebelled.

From Ramonet's point of view, globalization has been divided into various phases. The first was the stage of understanding the phenomenon, when intellectuals and the peoples of the world set about deciphering the globalization enigma – there is no doubt that the fall of the Soviet Union came out of the blue, it took the world by surprise. After a decade, from 1989 to 1999, the world moved on to a second phase, a phase of protest against the globalizing model. Once the phenomenon had been digested and understood, then came the protests against the model. From that point on, Ramonet argued in 2001, there had to be a move toward a third stage, that of an alternative proposal: this third phase is spreading throughout the world. The protests in Seattle, what happened in Quebec, in Genoa, were part of the protest phase. In this context he suggests that Venezuela is outside the pattern, because this country began to protest right from the start. In 1989 there was a widespread rebellion on the part of the people; in 1992 there was a military uprising and so, by 1998, while the world had hardly begun to protest, Venezuela had been protesting for a decade, and now an alternative model is under construction. Venezuela has been out in front, like a vanguard; this is Ramonet's thesis, which he has since been refining.

That conversation happened a few months prior to the coup; later, books began to be published about the Bolivarian process. There is one by Richard Gott, a British writer, *In the Shadow of the Liberator*. Another was published in Argentina, *Los sueños de Bolívar en la Venezuela de hoy* (Bolívar's Dreams in Today's Venezuela), by Carlos Aznarez. Another came out in Colombia, by Medófilo Medinas, *Chávez el elegido* (Chávez, The Chosen One). I don't like the title, but the book is good; this young author was from the Colombian Communist Party, although I don't think he is a member of the party any longer.

Books began to come out in Europe, particularly after the coup. This movement, which had already grown to some extent, began to flourish with Fidel's support. He has helped a lot in all of this; Cuba published a book with many of my speeches and talks and had it translated into English, German, Russian, and Vietnamese; It is all over the world.[10] One day, he said to me, "Gabo [Gabriel García Márquez] is going to be jealous, this book is in who-knows-how many editions by now."

Relations with Fidel

I call Fidel "brother," and he is like an older brother to me. A few months back Fidel sent me a handwritten message, maybe six double-sided pages long. After I read it, I set about replying; it took me a whole night and a day, on an old typewriter I have about the place. (Imagine, that at this level I'm using a typewriter, one I have had since I was a cadet, for some 30 years. I prefer using it to the computer, because of the sound of the keys, "Tack-tack-tack," like a dance, my fingers and ideas moving to a rhythm.) I wrote Fidel one particular sentence straight from my heart: I said that I had just read each of the six pages of his letter, and that I was now unsure whether to call him "brother" or "father." That's the kind of very special relationship I have with him, as you know.

We are in constant discussion. He gives me ideas — advice or otherwise, it doesn't matter what it is called. Some of his ideas could be called advice. Fidel has a particular theory of which he often speaks: that all that remains for these people is to kill me. He is always telling me to take care. When he came to Venezuela he said this in public, "Chávez is not taking care of himself." When he left, wherever I went, people in the street shouted to me, "Chávez, look after yourself, do you hear?" Fidel gave that order, he launched the slogan, "Take care of him;" "He doesn't take care of himself." Each time we meet he reminds me of it.

I called him the other night, at midnight, in January. I was in a

In this new phase, as president, they have clumsily tried to do the same thing. Once, at the end of January 1999, a few days before taking office, I went on a tour and arranged to stopover in Havana. Prior to that I had been to Buenos Aires, Brasilia, and Mexico. We were in Madrid. From Madrid we went to Paris, then on to Rome. From Rome we made a stopover in Venezuela, then Havana, and finally the Dominican Republic, which I left to the end and because it was closest. I wanted to visit before taking office. While we were waiting [in Madrid], one of my aides-de-camp told me Washington was on the line. We were having dinner with business people in Madrid, and I asked, "A call from Washington?" "Yes, it is Mr. Peter Romero." Romero was the under secretary of state for Ibero-American affairs, as it is called there. I picked up the phone immediately because he had been in Venezuela in December; he came with an invitation from President Clinton for me to travel to Washington. He wanted to know whether I had a visa because they had never given me one; they had always refused.

I picked up the phone and that man said, "Listen, president, we have found out that you are traveling to Havana."

I replied, "Yes, I am going to Havana in a few days' time."

On the spot he said to me, "Well, you know, we would advise against you going to Havana."

"What?"

"Yes, because if you were to go to Havana that would make it very difficult, you know, to get you an interview with President Clinton."

I was furious and said to him, "Listen here, Mr. Romero. You've got me all wrong. You are talking to the president of an independent country. Do me the favor of never raising this matter with me again. If you want to leave me a message I'll put my aide-de-camp on the line." And I did.

On the following day, in Paris, I announced to some journalists said, "You look like Chávez." The guy was young, I said, "I am Chávez. How are things?" I gave him my hand, he babbled two or three sentences, and continued on his way, but in the opposite direction. Suddenly, I heard a voice right behind me, "Chávez," and I turned around. I will never forget the expression on his face, "Chávez, Viva Fidel!"

That was the reply to the oligarchy's crassness. Viva Fidel! Those who tried to use the special relationship I have with Fidel to dirty my personal or political reputation, had not realized that instead they had only strengthened or refreshed it. They forgot that when Fidel came here in 1959 [just after the victory of the Cuban Revolution] it was the occasion of one of the biggest rallies in living memory. Down through all these decades our people have admired Fidel; they support him, they love him. I remember when Fidel attended the inauguration ceremony of Carlos Andrés Pérez, in 1989. Because I was working in Miraflores Palace, I saw the whole event. I remember the military parade, watching as the international guests were arriving. Everybody got off the buses, the middle-class in the assembly, the political hangers on, officials, adecos. They were all waiting for Fidel's arrival. When everyone had got off and Fidel hadn't appeared, an air of disappointment circulated in the assembly. They wanted to see him close up, just to look at him sitting there, watching the military parade. Fidel didn't turn up to the parade, for reasons to do with security, I imagine.

During the electoral campaign they brought out the 1994 video once again, attempting to confuse the people. The Venezuelan armed forces were given a video of the speeches Fidel and I made in Havana. They went from garrison to garrison handing out the video. Then a group of military psychologists warned them, "Christ! Put a stop to this! It's having the opposite effect; this video is stirring up admiration among the young soldiers for Fidel Castro and Chávez, for both of them, stop this."

Fidel and something I always thought was, my god, when I get out of here I have to meet Fidel. Thinking about the long years I was supposed to spend in jail, I thought, my god! Don't let him die. I wanted to meet him and when that day came, imagine what happened! I was invited to Cuba in December 1994. As you know, I went, and Fidel was waiting for me when the plane landed. I was surprised; I wanted very much to see him but I didn't expect to see him at the door of the plane, on a regular flight. That was when he gave me a hug, and the oligarchy here published the photo on the front pages, as I have already mentioned. I had never been on the front page before. Chávez on the front page? The photo was in color with per-verse headlines. They wrote quite a number of articles: "Fidel finishes off Chávez," "Chávez subordinate to Fidel," "The axis of evil," and so on. These mantras did not exist at the time, but they began to use this relationship, which was just establishing itself, in a diabolic and perverse way, to try to instill a fear of communism in our people, a fear of Fidel Castro, of dictatorship, and all such stories.

They devoted as much negative publicity as they possibly could to those two days I spent there. They broadcast a part of my speech in Havana on TV and invited some "experts" to comment. I returned to Venezuela two days later. It was December, Christmas had begun, and the streets were packed with people. I arrived in Maiquetía and a comrade and I took a taxi to the center of Caracas where we had a small office on loan to us from a lawyer friend, with a bit of furniture and little meeting room. I even used to sleep there.

Isea and I arrived and we got out into a semi-dark street. Remember that our people had been bombarded with images of the Fidel and Chávez embracing and who knows what else. A drunk was coming down the center of the street with a bottle in his hand, zigzagging. He was quite drunk, blind drunk, as we say here. I bumped into him, we were that close. I was trying to move to the other side of the street, to let him pass, but he was zigzagging along with his bottle. Then he quiet location, we were on the outskirts of Barinas, and we talked until it was almost dawn. The telephone became hot and there were problems with the line. Finally I said to him, "Listen, I have to rest for a while because I'm going to see my daughter." He knows her, Rosa Inés. Well, he knows all my children. "Ah! You're going to see your daughter," he remarked. "Yes, she is with her mother, that's where I'm going." He asked how far the trip was overland. "About three hours," I told him. Fidel was pensive for a moment. "Three hours, that's quite far, but you go overland if you can."

He has said to me on a number of occasions that he had constantly warned Omar Torrijos, "Don't travel in those light aircraft so much, Omar." Omar ended up dying in the mountains. So, I do believe he is looking after me. One night we were having dinner when he suddenly asked me, as if thinking out loud, "Well, and what are you eating?" I had just started eating some fish and salad, though I don't really like lettuce. He was eating and looking at me sideways, and I heard him clearly when he changed his tone. "Your diet." Another evening I began to smoke and suddenly he said, "That's three cigarettes, Chávez, three, and another one makes four." He is on the ball about all of this, or the wine, "Red wine is good for the circulation, a glass a day is good for you." He gives me advice about my diet, whether something has too much fat in it, about types of deep-sea fish, about cold-water versus warm-water fish. For a while he was sending me ice cream until the doctors conducted some blood tests. When he found out that my cholesterol levels were high he said, "There was I sending you ice cream, with your high cholesterol." So yes, ideas, advice, we really do have a lovely relationship, very special, infinitely respectful.

This relationship began quite some time ago, dating back to my time in prison when I read *Face to Face with Fidel Castro*, "History Will Absolve Me,"[11] *Fidel and Religion*, by Frei Betto,[12] and the one by Gianni Miná, *An Encounter with Fidel*.[13] I read many books about what had taken place. That night, in the hotel, Romero phoned and I spoke to him. He said, "Mr. President, you misunderstood me. I didn't mean to say that to you. President Clinton will meet with you."

"Oh, okay, but tell the president that if he cannot meet me it doesn't matter. By the way, I am going to Havana, that is not debatable and nobody should raise the matter with me again. I will not accept you or anyone else raising it," I said to him.

I went to Havana and two days later I was with Clinton in the White House. My team included some members who ended up joining the opposition, such as Luis Michelena. They were constantly worried that I would mention Fidel Castro in my speeches, in radio interviews or on TV. They told me it wasn't necessary to mention Fidel so often. But in this regard I don't have a guilty conscience at all.

In Monterrey [at the Summit of the Americas], I was furious when Bush, in Fidel's absence, launched an attack against Cuba and Fidel in his inauguration speech. When it was my turn to speak, as I have already mentioned, I said that in Venezuela in 2003, in spite of the fact that the subject [of the summit] was growth with equality, there had been no economic growth. Economic growth had fallen by at least 10 percent, because of the coup and sabotage of the oil industry. There was an economic recession. Nevertheless, thanks to Cuba's invaluable support, Venezuela had experienced an expansion in social welfare, equality, and social justice through, for example, Mission Robinson. It was the least I could do, and I did it.

They told me Bush was burning with anger. I was not looking at him, but afterwards I was told he turned red and sat motionless in his chair. I had mentioned Cuba three times. I had thanked the Cuban people and Fidel for their support. I have no regrets about that, but I am sorry that others do. That is what Gaddafi said to me when I told him by telephone what had happened in Monterrey. He asked why

Cuba had not been at the meeting for the entire continent of the Americas, "Ah well! That's because the United States excluded Cuba." He said to me, "Listen Hugo, on one occasion here in Africa, the British tried to prevent Mugabe, the president of Zimbabwe, attending a European Union meeting. We said that if Mugabe didn't go then nobody would. Latin America should do the same." But see how they coerce and manipulate us.

It is the least we can do, and without regrets. I am honored by Fidel's friendship and each time I feel this in my soul, I express it. I am grateful to him, not for me, but for my people. Fidel's determination to cooperate with us is unprecedented. I don't believe that a precedent of this kind exists between any other president and a people that is not their own people. Furthermore, this cooperation is permanent, solid, and on the increase.

Children and grandchildren

As you have seen, I have a large family. I have four children, but I also have millions more. All these children here belong, in part, to me. Our poet, Andrés Eloy Blanco, said, "He who has a child, has all the children in the world." In my eyes, these 18- and 20-year-old girls are like daughters to me. As are these 18-year-old boys, neighborhood kids, out there playing baseball. However, about my own children, I have four of my own flesh and blood. I also have two grandchildren, a boy and a girl. The girl is at school.

Unfortunately, I don't have much time to devote to my family; the reality is that they devote their time to me. My father comes here from time to time, as does my mother. Sometimes, but not often, I manage to come home; of course there is very tight security in the surroundings. My grown-up children live here. Just recently, Rosa got married and went to live with her husband in an apartment. I see them from time to time. They visit me at the White Palace.

In one way or another they are involved in the revolutionary process, some more than others. María Gabriela is the most involved – she is studying at university and she gives me information and ideas. She enjoys it a lot. Rosa less so, although she does take part. Hugo, even less so; he is the one who has most suffered the complications of all of this. And Rosa Inés is six years old, though sometimes she wears her red beret.

I know that they love me and understand the revolutionary

process. My son is the most rebellious, even though he hasn't fully understood it; and out of the girls, Rosa understands, has taken it on board, although María has too, but much more so. From the time she was a little girl, María learned very quickly. I remember when they came to visit me in prison, Rosa cried, while María arrived happy, she flew in, jumping up and down. They have two very different personalities; when Rosa was growing up and had her first period, she was afraid to tell me. It was her mother who told me and she was lying down in her room and I had to go in and comfort her and say, "Oh, sweetheart!" etc. María, on the other hand, came running into my cell when I was a prisoner and told me about it with no hang-ups.

Right now Rosa is 24 years old, María is 22, Hugo is 20, and Rosa Inés is 6.

When I was in prison María was 12 years old, she was born in 1980. She wrote well. I remember one day she gave me a letter she had written. It was beautiful, "For Papi, my loving father." At 12 years old:

> My loving father. Papá, now I finally understand why you used to arrive home at night worn-out, and why you bored us sitting there reading "Oración a Simón Bolívar en la noche negra de América" (A Prayer to Simón Bolívar in the black night of the Americas).

(That is a poem by Mafud Maziz, a Chilean poet. I placed the poem on the main wall and from time to time I would read it to them in the evenings.)

> Now, Papá, I finally know why there were trips to the beach without towels and bathing suits, "Let's go, let's go, get in" and off we would go; there was always a power boat, an island, and young people hiding out there [a way of describing quick escapes].

That's how she came to understand it. One day, while I was in prison and we were talking in the tiny room, she said to me, "Papá, one day when we are on the bus with Mamí, I would like to shout out loud, 'I am *comandante* Chávez's daughter!'" She is the one who identifies most with all of this. She writes well, as I have said, and I encourage her to write, to read, something she really enjoys. She is a follower of Che to the death, and a rabid Fidelista.

On the day of the coup I called her. I managed to talk to Rosa, who was with María. Rosa was crying, crying nonstop, she could barely talk; she was hiding in her boyfriend's house, who is now her husband, by the beach. When we had spoken for a short while she said María was there and put her on the line. María is much steadier, and she asked me, kind of jokingly, "Where are you, Papá?" I said, "Listen, darling, I'm a prisoner again."

"Well, Papá, so you're a prisoner again?" It was as if she was saying, "Christ, how long is this going to go on for?"

I said to her, "María, María, listen to me, start calling anyone and everyone, and tell them that I have been taken prisoner, that I have not resigned, and that I am not going to resign either. María, listen, they could kill me here." It seemed clear that they were going to kill me because they were reading my resignation on the TV.

"The president resigns;" "Chávez has gone." There it was, though the signature was not mine. One of the lieutenants guarding me had lent me a tiny TV where I was being held prisoner. Obviously, when I saw that, I said to myself, I'm a dead man. I asked the lieutenant to get me a telephone and I called and kept on calling and finally got in touch with my daughters. María phoned Fidel, and when she got him on the line she told him I had been taken prisoner. That was when Fidel decided to include her in the Round Table discussions with some journalists.[14]

Fidel called her a heroine, and just imagine it, she felt like a real heroine.

The war in Iraq

The war in Iraq is a result of Washington's irrationality and inability to grasp what is going on in the world. The best example of this is here in Venezuela, when the coup d'état took place with the support of Washington. They completely misunderstood the situation. They are entirely mistaken in their grasp of what is happening in the world.

In Washington they thought that by overthrowing Chávez and establishing a transitional government in Venezuela, as they call it, they could guarantee oil supply, as if it were as simple as drinking a glass of water. They got a massive shock, just like what has happened to them in Iraq. They thought that by invading Iraq, putting tanks into the very heart of Baghdad, pulling down the statue of Saddam, and installing a government of military occupation, everything would be alright. What this shows is the lack of understanding of what a people is, the Iraqi people or any other people.

We, of course, have been against the war from the very outset; we have always said we are in favor of self-determination and national independence. Now, there is no use crying over spilt milk. No matter how much we oppose the war and argue in favor of respect for humanity and for the rights of a people, the forces of occupation are there reminding us that this is not happening. The question now is to ask oneself how all of this can be sorted out, how the situation in Iraq can be resolved. Maybe the United Nations could take control, but it is unlikely; if they didn't manage to do it before the war then it is even less likely now. Perhaps through international pressure, though this has decreased, or internal pressure applied by the people of United States themselves, although this has also decreased. There was a point when it became quite strong but then it lessened. The question we should be asking is whether it is possible to reactivate some factors to the extent that the United States and Britain will be forced to withdraw from Iraq. I don't see that happening, at least for the next few months. I think the military occupation will continue. I don't believe that the United States will make a decision to withdraw, no matter how many bodies are brought back from that region.

There is one chance, and that is if the people of the United States unleash their protest against Bush's government and the war, using a variety of means, like the public demonstrations of last year or during the Vietnam War, or to wait for the November elections. They could usher in a scenario that would force a change of policy toward Iraq. That is quite unlikely. Iraq is becoming a Vietnam, not in the jungle, but in the desert.

I think that this is a painful lesson. We don't want dead bodies, civilians or innocent children. Neither do we want dead Iraqi or US soldiers; we don't want anyone dead. Nevertheless, there is a resistance movement, and deaths are occurring almost every day. The attacks are reaching monstrous levels, with bombs in hotel entrances where US citizens are staying, and at the entrances of military bases. This is a people engaged in resistance and a people who are naturally warriors; they have a history of war that dates back centuries from the time of Mesopotamia and all those empires. It is a lesson. Those who aim to dominate the world now found themselves in the deserts of Iraq, facing the resistance of the Iraqi people.

It is a lesson for the imperialists, just like the resistance of the Venezuelan people was during those days in April. Like the dignified response of the patriotic generals and soldiers of the presidential guard who refused to swear loyalty to Carmona. One soldier asked, "Who is this old guy? Where is my President Chávez?" Another soldier said, "We are not swearing loyalty to him." And they did not swear loyalty to Carmona, in spite of the fact that he came out wearing a tricolor sash. Finally a colonel arrived and said, "Señor Carmona, you are under arrest. Take off the sash," and they took him prisoner. These are the dignified responses that allow us to believe in a different world, where there are no more empires. Let's hope so!

An ALBA against the FTAA

We have always expressed our disagreement to the Free Trade Area of the Americas (FTAA). It is counter to the core issues contained in our constitution. We cannot sign an FTAA agreement without violating our constitution.

The FTAA is an abuse of sovereignty; it is a colonial, imperialist plan. We are a part of the FTAA because, when we came to power, Venezuela was already in the so-called Summit of the Americas, but from the first day, in Quebec, we have been very firm. Of course, at that time we were on our own, Venezuela was alone in its position at that summit. Some presidents of some small countries were with us. I remember comments made to me in the corridors during those days in 2000, comments akin to acknowledgment, "Your speech and your warnings were very good."

I asked some of them why they hadn't spoken, "If that's what you feel, why don't you say it out there?"

"No, Mr. President, we don't have oil, we are tiny." The power of the empire to conduct blackmail is barbaric. Sometimes all that is required is a telephone call from Washington to undermine a government, a simple telephone call.

That blackmail doesn't work with us, and not just because of the oil. I said to the friend who made that remark, "Listen, even if Venezuela didn't have oil, we would still hold the same position. This is not about oil, it's about taking a position in defense of your country's interests."

Now, insofar as we have made progress, we face a different situation. Now we have other countries in the continent that, although they may not be exactly aligned with our position, are very close to us.

This is the case of Brazil, where for example a "light" version of the FTAA has been put forward, which I call FTAA-Lite.[15] Certain positions have been adopted there, particularly by Lula, because Lula is Lula. Lula is an unwavering man with very clear ideas, and of course there is a difficult situation there in which you have to separate the man from the circumstances. Something similar is happening in Argentina; they have come much closer to our position. This is also the case with the Caricom,[16] almost in its entirety. The Caribbean region has grasped that the FTAA is capable of destroying its possibilities for development. So, I believe that the FTAA will not be able to proceed. The last FTAA meeting in Puebla, barely a week ago, ended without result. At this point in time, the FTAA has been defeated. Nonetheless, the battle against it must continue to be waged, particularly the battle for an alternative.

We have discussed this with Fidel. An idea crossed my mind — a bit of mischief on my part — which I'll explain as quickly as I can.

The Caribbean Summit was held here in Margarita, on December 10, 2001. By coincidence, Fidel and our friends from the Caribbean arrived at the time of the first employers' strike [the oil strike]. Fidel arrived in a good mood on that day. I had taken part in four events throughout the entire country because it was the national day of the air force. I had been far away to the plains region, to hand over land and to proclaim the land act. Having done all of that, I traveled to Margarita to wait for Fidel, who arrived 15 minutes afterwards, around midnight. He was wearing his uniform and had a broad grin on his face. I asked him, "Why are you so happy?" He replied that he was envious, "An employers' strike, marvelous." We hardly slept that night. During the summit it occurred to me, as a bit of playfulness on my part, to condemn the FTAA and suggest ALBA, meaning dawn in Spanish; I was playing around with the letters.

A dawn: an ALBA against the FTAA. ALBA stands for the Bolivarian Alternative for the Americas. The summit ended and all of them left; about a week later I received a request from Fidel in which he asked me to send him the ALBA document. I asked him, "What document," I didn't have anything. Nevertheless, we have been working on a proposal, which is now taking shape. I am going to keep stressing the point, for example, in Brazil, and with other countries too, but of course Brazil is the giant of South America.

Just imagine the importance of a "PetroAmerica." Venezuela has PDVSA; Brazil has PETROBRAS; Colombia has COPETROL; Trinidad has PETROTRIN. Each of these are 100 percent state-owned; fortunately they were never privatized. Ecuador has PETRO-ECUADOR and Peru has PETROPERU. Bolivia has huge gas potential, which was one of the causes of the crisis that got rid of Sánchez de Losada. Imagine this arch running from the north of South America, all these countries with immense oil and gas reserves. Imagine PetroAmerica, a kind of Latin American OPEC. Obviously the political will is required, but this is a serious proposal for an alternative model of integration. The outcome of my mischief in Margarita, this would be called ALBA: the Bolivarian alternative.

We have also thought about building a Latin American military defense force. Such a military force seems like a dream, but who knows whether at some point further on it might be possible. There is potential for collaboration in sectors such as iron and steel, too. For example, Cuba has nickel mines. The fusion of nickel and steel produces stainless steel, and we have steel here. In this, Cuba and Venezuela are working along the same lines. Hopefully we will soon be able to reach a joint agreement about steel and nickel investments, because the fact of the matter is that at the end of the day, Venezuela is purchasing stainless steel.

Likewise with aluminum. We sell aluminum in rods and bars and then we buy back aluminum airplanes, cutlery, cups, tables, chairs, and countless other things. Why? Because we have not added surplus value to production. This would be one of the key elements for an alternative development model in Latin America, from an economic point of view. This would be the ALBA.

"If there is a referendum
we will win it anyway..."

In relation to the Recall Referendum, I am certain that the signatures "collected," are not real. There is already evidence, for example, of some people signing twice. Around 60,000 sheets of paper have "disappeared" from the desks; they were taken away and then presented, a month later, to the National Electoral Council. Last night I was handed the petition—it would have been great for you to see it. They are still processing it and now is not the right time to make that document public, but the time will come. So, last night I was given copies of the signed sheets; a single individual had completed them. Imagine! Just one person filling out the sheet with false signatures, using the identity card numbers of people who have died or are minors.

We will publish all of this. Last night, in a meeting about this, I said at one point that the opposition had disappointed me. When the figure for obtaining a Recall Referendum was established it was done to facilitate things; we did not establish a formula to make the calling of a Recall Referendum impossible... The Recall Referendum formula is our proposal. We drew up certain criteria, such as obtaining signatures from 20 percent of the electorate, which is not an impossible figure.

Three years ago, at the last election, 2.8 million people voted against me. You might assume that as the number of voters has increased, this figure would have increased as well — more young people have registered — but it didn't grow proportionally. We won a million extra votes, a million and a bit.

The collection of signatures to call a referendum took four days; if 2.8 million people voted against me in one day, in four days they could have easily collected 2.4 million signatures [or 20 percent of the electorate]. I always said, let's work on the basis that they will be able to collect the signatures, if they are well organized and considering they have the advantage of the media on their side. But with all the money that they have here, plus that which Washington sends — as was revealed a short time ago, through receipts and everything — they couldn't get the signatures. Honestly, they have disappointed me. I thought they were going to collect them legally for the referendum.

Now that is not the problem; the problem is that being unable to get the signatures legally, they have engaged in a whole series of fraudulent measures, such as signing more than once, in full knowledge that it was likely they would be caught out, because we were all going to be on the alert. They got a substantial number of people to sign twice or even three times; even the deceased signed. I have a list of deceased going back 20 years whose signatures are on the list. Underage children signed and they took the sheets abroad to Venezuelans living outside of the country. That was forbidden; they had to come and sign here.

Now we have the list, including passport details and so on, of those people living in New York who appear on the referendum petition as if they were living here. Their names are on the records, as are the names of those who spent time in New York collecting signatures. So now you have an idea of what they got up to. Their goal was very clear, and we always understood that they were going to hand the signatures over. I even thought they were going to get more, because they had said, "We're going to hand over five million signatures."

In the end, they handed over 3.4 million signatures; in other words, a million more than necessary. Their idea was to deliver more signatures than was necessary, because it would be very difficult for the National Electoral Council to scrutinize so many signatures, to deprive them of 3.4 million signatures. That's why now the National Electoral Council is preparing to scutinize and to remove the signatures that have to be removed, which, I am certain is over a million. I had my doubts, but now I am sure. Because now I have seen it all.

Is there any chance the National Electoral Council will evade its responsibility to check all the signatures and remove those that are invalid? I would say that yes, there is a chance, but it is minimal. There is a group of people in the council who are very honorable, who are prepared to take any necessary decisions and to ensure that the electoral laws, which the commission itself established before the signatures were collected, are respected.

By way of conclusion, I would therefore say that the most likely outcome, from my point of view and from an objective position free of any pressure on our part, is that the National Electoral Council will rule that not enough signatures have been collected, even though they might be subject to pressure or even to death threats.

Remember that the Supreme Court ruled by a one-vote majority that there had not been a coup d'état here. I had to swallow the ruling that I had not been taken prisoner, but that I was only under guard, etc. The day they made this decision and announced to the world that there had not been a coup d'état in Venezuela, I had to swallow the whole story. And take note, there were no deaths or disappearances here as a result of that ruling…

The situation now is much more difficult; it is very unlikely that there will be a referendum. Instead, it is highly possible that some opposition sectors will lose their cool and try to force the country into violence, but I am telling you now what I have said in public, as a warning: that the tolerant, infinitely flexible Hugo Chávez has been left behind, he's gone.

When the coup took place some of the top military brass in power crossed over to join the traitors, and others remained indecisive out of fear. In spite of the fact that I had given them an order to hold back the mass of people who were heading toward to Miraflores Palace — and there were numerous ways to hold them back with no one getting killed — they didn't want to do it, because this clash was part of the coup plan. Now, the situation is different: the top ranks of the armed forces are loyal and willing to carry out all orders as instructed. In any case I hope, indeed I am more than hopeful, that we have greatly improved our intelligence services and are capable detecting and analyzing the reality. There is the chance that these people will provoke further violent outbreaks, but I don't for a moment believe that they will again drive us into the state of heightened tension and violence that placed us on the absolute defensive between April and December 2002.

I don't think there will be a referendum, though there will be other problems we will have to face as steadfastly as we can. I think that the majority of the country, including the opposition, does not want violence. Some have learned the lesson. The business sector let itself be led along the path toward sabotage and it doesn't want to find itself there again. We know that what these people want is to work, produce, and recover their losses, because they lost quite a lot during the strike and no one has repaid them. The real manipulators of the coup have left the country and they don't answer to anyone. I think that many in the middle class became tired of so many marches, promises that Chávez was leaving or about to leave any moment, when he never left. I believe some of them have realized that they were being used as pawns, as cannon fodder. I think that today the country is in a much more promising situation. But in any case, we have our eyes and ears open.

So, if there is a referendum, we will win it. Why am I so sure? It is a question of simple mathematics. The fact is, in a referendum, in order for them to able to revoke my mandate, they require at least one vote more than the 3.8 million votes I got in 2003. Though they say that in four days they collected 3.4 million signatures, I am convinced that a count wouldn't even provide a figure of 2.2 million. It's just not possible for them to get 3.8 million, plus the one vote more than I got in a single day.

The forthcoming presidential elections for the new six-year term of office will be held in December 2006, followed by those of 2012. That government would then have the responsibility of handing over government in 2013. The idea then is consolidation, and we have a lot going for us, although there are many national and international threats. But at a national level, I feel that things are on our side. There may even be major changes taking place on the continent this year, in the United States, and among many other governments and new forces emerging.

The idea right now is to consolidate this project in the nine years that remain; to strengthen our institutions; to finish burying what has to be buried, as Gramsci said when describing crises. In other words, when something is dying it doesn't simply die. At the same time, something is being born but neither is it actually born. We have to finish burying what has to die and give birth to what has to be born. We are still a long way from this. That's my challenge; though it's not my personal challenge. I always say that I am not the president; I don't feel superior to the next person. I am simply Hugo, but without denying that now, as president, this implies something else.

While talking to Fidel on one occasion, he asked me, "What have you been doing, Chávez?"

"I have just arrived from some place; I walked around for a while, and talked to the people. And you?" I asked him.

"The same, almost the same." Then he said to me, "Do you know what we are? The fact is that we are not presidents, Chávez, we are two regular guys, who like to hang out." He is right. Fidel hit the nail on the head. I am not a president or anything else. I am a guy who likes to hang out.

I am a happy man. I am happy because I feel I am fulfilling a dream I have had for many years, since I was young. I am happy and I see a great future for Venezuela. Not just for Venezuela but for all of Latin America. I think that this must be the century, as Simón Rodríguez used to say, "Thomas Mann's utopia is here in America, in South America." That's the way he put it, and I do believe that this century is our century. We are no longer Fanon's wretched of the earth. We have to be, like Bolívar, the new type of human being, the link between Africans and indigenous peoples, Americans, Europeans. Che spoke about the "new man" and I believe that the time has come. Enough words have been said, enough fighting has occurred, enough disasters have taken place. The failures are over and done with, I feel sure of this and happy about it. I feel optimistic because, as my grandmother used to say, you can smell the wind of change, it is in the air.

Once the interview was over, when I was gathering my things, I saw Chávez's legs under the glass table and I realized they weren't hairy. I asked him jokingly if he was hairless,[17] *to which he replied, "As you can see, we indigenous people are hairless, even though I am a little whiter and have moles. A woman once asked me if I shaved my legs and I said, 'No! Hairs don't grow on my legs!'"*

So, with laughter and camaraderie, the interview ended and we departed, leaving a little of our affection with him. We left without saying good-bye, only, until next time.

Epilogue

Before returning to Cuba I met with a very special woman, Noeli Pocaterra, vice-president of the National Assembly. Noeli Pocaterra is from the Wayúu community, one of the ethnic indigenous groups that inhabited our continent before the Spanish conquerors arrived. They retain their culture, language, and spiritual beliefs today, traditions that have resisted over 500 years of exploitation and humiliation.

We had a lengthy conversation, some of which I would like to share. It was an unforgettable experience. We first met in Maracaibo and I already was aware of her work in defense of her people, but to have the opportunity of talking personally for a while was wonderful; deep within me I felt the greatness of our peoples.

Noeli described how it has been very difficult for her to accept the Christian religion and its highly individualistic theories, even regarding the origins of life. Her beliefs, on the other hand, are based on collective legends. She told of the Earth Goddess who ignored the Rain God. One day he became so angry with her that he produced a powerful lightning bolt. When the Earth Goddess heard the noise she was frightened and looked at the Rain God, who interpreted the look as her consent, and flooded the world with water, which is why the first plants were born shortly afterwards. Still not happy, the Rain God decided to flood the earth with his sap, and that is how the first Wayúu people came into being. All Wayúu emerged from Mother

Earth at the same time. According to legend, the first head to emerge was that of a woman, so that's why women carry the burden of pro-creation.

Obviously, there is much more to this, but I was struck by the tenderness and strength the Wayúu attach to their origins; all of them together, classless, mutually respectful, with important social obligations for those elected by the community as its representatives, but with equality of rights for everyone. How wonderful it would be if all of us understood this message; what a lesson!

Mamacita, Noeli's other name, described a meeting that took place between Hugo Chávez, who was then a military captain, and a group of indigenous people in a village he had been assigned to. When the local inhabitants saw a military vehicle arriving they would hide immediately; their experience had never been pleasant. But one day they couldn't hide a group of children playing with a sheep that had been covered in grease. They decided to remain out of sight close by, if necessary, to help the children. They were taken aback when a young soldier got out of the vehicle and walked over to the children, taking one up into his arms and cleaning him up a little. The villagers felt there was no danger, and little by little came out and approached the soldier, who had brought an interpreter with him to communicate in their language.

Chávez, the soldier, asked for some water, but nobody moved or said anything; the translator tried again to communicate with the villagers and to ask for water. One of them decided to explain that they didn't have any glasses and didn't know how to bring water to him. Chávez replied that they could give him a gourd; he would drink it however they did. Shortly afterwards, they decided to go hunting together, at Chávez's request using their arrows, and returned to cook the food together.

In the afternoon, Chávez insisted on showing a group of them where they could find him, should they need him for whatever reason. He showed them the garrison and the house where he lived. His presence was required on several occasions: at that time, certain white people had made a sport out of hunting indigenous people. They shot them below the waist and cut off their ears for hunting trophies. Of course these murderers got off scot-free, they were treated with impunity; no one pressed charges. Who was going to listen to indigenous peoples' complaints? Nobody.

This community has its own laws that allow forgiveness in exchange for something. But the white men never offered anything to mitigate the outrages. And if a member of the community decided to take a pig or whatever as a token of forgiveness, they were accused of stealing and punished accordingly, meaning that they were sentenced to prison, in addition to being the victim of injustice. During the time Chávez was there, he tried to protect them by appealing to the law. At least that is the way those who lived through that period tell it; not only did they respect him, they cared for him too because he defended their community.

In a short period of time I learned a lot from Mamacita. I strongly feel the need to become better acquainted with my roots, to know more about these peoples who have so bravely preserved their culture so that we can learn to respect our land and our fellow compatriots more. Perhaps because of this, it is painful to acknowledge the ignominy in which they still live, practically ignored in this world of ours.

During my short stay in Venezuela — a sister country that is different and yet the same — I had the privilege of meeting extraordinary individuals, from young people to those with immense experience, from ministers to peasant farmers and indigenous peoples; in short, a whole range of Venezuelans.

I visited the hills of Caracas and spent time with Cuban doctors and their patients, men and women who had always found it difficult to get medical care because they lived in remote regions and, as was almost always the case, because medical fees were high. They now have doctors living with them in their community. When patients miss their scheduled appointments, the medical staff fetch them. Very often the doctors and nurses are treated as part of the family, such is their degree of integration into the community.

Thousands of stories emerged during these conversations, such as that of the young Cuban doctor who was mugged in the street and arrived home in tears. The neighbors got involved immediately, and in no time they found and returned what was stolen from her. They also asked her to use her white coat whenever she went out so that she could be identified as a Cuban doctor, stressing that this would never happen to her again.

I also spent some time with teachers who are confronting the task of teaching their fellow citizens and raising their level of education and culture. I visited several former political police barracks, where torture used to be carried out, and which today are being transformed into senior high school classrooms.

I had the opportunity to learn about new housing projects, about cooperatives, and to talk to the young, highly enthusiastic people involved in social work. In other words, I got a glimpse of the revolutionary process that is underway, that still has a long way to go, and that needs the respect and solidarity of all of us. We are all of us bound in one way or another to the struggle for a better world, and the Bolivarian Republic of Venezuela is a living example of the fact that when a people decide to take control of their destiny and fight for it, they can make their dreams come true.

Let's fight for these dreams so that in the not-so-distant future they become reality; let's struggle together. Ever onward to victory!

Aleida Guevara
Havana, 2004

Appendices

Appendix One
A Guevaran "Aló Presidente"

We left Caracas early on the morning of Sunday, February 8, 2004, and arrived in Maracaibo without any hitches. During the journey I spoke with several people [in the Bolivarian government], each of whom a book could be written about, something we will have to leave for another occasion. On our arrival we joined a motorcade and headed to where the TV program "Aló Presidente" was to be filmed. There was a sea of happy people, full of hope and anxious to be closer in order to greet their president.

The "Aló Presidente" episode for that day was devoted to youth. Reference was made to the battle of La Victoria that took place on February 12, 1814, when the republic fell. Chávez reflected on the battle and in this discussion he brought up the subject of Che Guevara.

HUGO CHÁVEZ: Che Guevara said, very clearly, that in order for a revolutionary process to be successful, it must motivate the people and retain their motivation; without this it would not be a revolution.

That is what happened to Bolívar until the year 1814; the Venezuelan people defeated Bolívar in 1814, there is no question about it. The point is that Bolívar had the greatness required to reflect on the defeat, to understand it, and then to go back and unite with the black and olive-skinned Venezuelans, the people of the plains; he won the people's support, their admiration. He removed from himself all vestiges of the oligarch he had been, the *mantuano*, and joined with the marginalized sectors of society. As the poet said, he ended up with his feet firmly on the ground; he ended up like José Martí, "Sharing my destiny with the poor of my land."

I am talking about this in very general terms, as a strategic orientation for today's battle. The people, the Venezuelan people, are very dynamic. I refer to Ernesto Che Guevara for many reasons, but one of them is that Aleida Guevara, a daughter of Ernesto Guevara, is here visiting us today. Aleida is a pediatrician and a researcher; she is Cuban and last night we spent a while talking, two hours or more (perhaps more because she is a good conversationalist). After the formal interview, a project she is working on with her team, we spent some time talking together. She told me some stories about her father she remembers from when she was five years old.

Aleida, we open our hearts to you and say, welcome to this land that belongs to you, to your father, to Cuba, and to all of these people. How are you?

ALEIDA GUEVARA: Well.

HC: You're well? How do you feel this morning? Did you get some rest?

AG: Yes, of course, very well, ready for the fight.

HC: For the fight! Are you familiar with Maracaibo?

AG: No and unfortunately I won't have time to get to know it and enjoy it. That's something I'll have to leave for another time.

HC: But you could spend an afternoon here, and tour Limpia and La Cañada, couldn't you? Noeli [Pocaterra], who's not from this country, is there. Noeli, you could take Aleida to Guajira, couldn't you?

NOELI POCATERRA: Of course, why not? I would be very pleased to; in fact I have already mentioned it. But if Aleida leaves with you this afternoon, we will have to bring her back, because she is very interested in traditional medicine.

HC: Ah! And the children; last night my grandson held on to her and didn't want to let go. Right?

AG: Right.

HC: The little rascal is very cute.

AG: Very cute.

HC: It seems he fell in love with you, something like what you thought happened with that man; you told your mother you believed he was in love with you. Imagine that. What a lovely story! Could you tell us about it?

AG: Yes, no problem. That was when Papi returned to Cuba on his way back from the Congo, in order to train for Bolivia. He entered Cuba without our people being aware of it, disguised as "Old Ramón." He wanted to say farewell to his children. We went to see this man, but we didn't know he was our father. After dinner, I fell over and hit my head. My father gathered me up in his arms; he was a doctor so he checked me over, felt my head. I sensed something [when he held me], because a little while later I tried to tell my mother a secret, which I then repeated in a loud voice, "Mamá, I think this man is in love with me." Of course, I didn't know he was my father, but I did know he had spoken to me with such tenderness. He was capable of conveying his affection without words.

Later on, during my adolescence, I searched my memory for all these recollections. I finally said to myself, well, he's not with us but I know that he loved us, and that he was a man with dignity, true to his ideas.

I read a newspaper editorial here saying that my father would not be on Chávez's side. I would really like to point out that we, I am talking about my people, have always grown up with Che's presence.

There are many Cubans here today, side by side with the Bolivarian people. They are Che Guevara's sons and daughters, so Che is present in the dignity of all those Cuban doctors [working here].

HC: Those who die for life cannot be called dead. Let's greet all the Che Guevaras who are here, the Cuban doctors, the hundreds of women doctors who are on Mission Barrio Adentro. How are you comrades? The Venezuelan people embrace you and offer you their gratitude. Today and forever, Barrio Adentro!

We are listening to Aleida Guevara. There is the unmistakable face of one of the greatest revolutionaries in the history of the Americas and the world, Ernesto Guevara, a man loyal to his ideas.

Che once wrote, "In a true revolution, you win or you die," and that's the way it is; you win or you die. That's where the slogan "Homeland or Death" comes from, which we have combined with the slogan of the patriot José Félix Ribas, who said to his troops just before the decisive moment at the battle of La Victoria, "Long Live the Republic!" Many of them were young scholars, students at the University of Caracas, young people who didn't know how to handle a rifle but who had formed an army in an attempt to stop Bobes and the violence that was coming at them full speed. There comes Bobes; we can't choose between victory or death, we have to be victorious. "Long live the Republic!"

We say the same today, we cannot be defeated, we cannot fail, we are under obligation to win. That is why we say we will be victorious.

AG: But there is another saying by Che, which is very important for me, because it is the proof that you have to keep going forward. He bade farewell to the Cuban people saying, "Homeland or Death," but also, "Ever Onward to Victory." We will always fight on until we achieve victory; I think these words are what have made the most impact on us.

HC: This is the path, victory, ever onward to victory. What a coincidence, the battle that we have been talking about took place in a village called La Victoria, the victory. And José Félix Ribas said that we cannot choose between victory or death.

So then, welcome to Aleida, and to all your team, your comrades and friends; this is your homeland too, friend and sister.

When the televised part of "Aló Presidente" was over, Chávez called me over to the microphone.

HC: Listen Aleida, come and listen to this. Your father once said, "Today the struggle; tomorrow belongs to us." But it belongs to all of you now. We said this in the 1960s and 1970s: today the struggle; the future belongs to us. Sometimes I say, and I don't mean to be pessimistic, that they stole the future from us. We lived through the 1960s, the 1970s, the 1980s, the 1990s, and we reached 2000, the magic date, and where is the future? They stole it from us.

AG: We are building it.

HC: Exactly, building it, but now it is not for us.

AG: Yes, it is for us as well, it is our fruit. We sowed it for new generations.

HC: That's true. Let's talk more about your daughters and my grandson who you carried in your arms. How old are they?

AG: Fifteen and thirteen.

HC: What are they called?

AG: Estefanía and Celia.

HC: And your mother?

AG: Aleida, I am named after her.

HC: A girl of 70.

AG: Don't say that, she'll kill us!

HC: Thank you, my dear.

On our return to Caracas we spoke for a few minutes about smoking habits and discussed some of the wide-ranging subjects he had broached during his conversation with the people. Furthermore, we agreed on a date for the next interview and that is where we met once again.[1]

Appendix Two
Interview with General Jorge García Carneiro

The relationship between the armed forces
and the Bolivarian movement

First and foremost I want to make something clear about my position during the time I was commander of the Third Division and military garrison in Caracas, which covers the states of Vargas and Miranda. There was no direct relationship between the armed forces and the Fifth Republic Movement (MVR). It was simply that we, through a series of decisions, found a new way to guide the armed forces along the path of national development. Remember that the armed forces have two key roles to fulfill: the security and the defense of this country, and its sovereignty in terms of territory, that is land, sea and air; these are their main duties.

There is a secondary mission that the constitution of the Bolivarian Republic of Venezuela has assigned to them, which is participation in national development. For this reason the armed forces includes units such as the sixth engineers' corps, which has teams of engineering experts working in the construction of railways. This is one of the missions being promoted by the government. It is clear, for example, that the development of a country requires an inexpensive, efficient, and fast transportation system that, in one way or another, improves the quality of life in the villages it passes through. We are supporting repair work in schools, outpatient clinics, and sports arenas, with the aim of improving the quality of life in these neighborhoods. We also take part in humanitarian projects, such as medical or surgical procedures, particularly because of delays or bad management in some of the hospitals.

In other words, due to a lack of resources, or possibly because of negligence or poor administration, a series of needs have arisen among the population, that have required us to develop, through humanitarian missions, operations that directly target the poorest, neediest classes who, obviously, have suffered the most.

This is why the Venezuelan people identify more with the revolutionary movement. Explained simply, it is like this: during the past 40 years or so the armed forces were shut away in their garrisons. They were heavily criticized. Soldiers, for example, were called parasites, who were paid a good salary but did nothing to earn it. Nevertheless, this government knows the abilities and potential of the armed forces and is conscious of its vast infrastructure extending throughout the national territory and its awesome capacity to respond. This is possibly because at the heart of the government is a particular individual, the president of the republic.

In this way, a plan was developed and coordinated that was initially called Plan Bolívar 2000. Then humanitarian work was added to its goals, which involved the armed forces in caring for the neediest sector. The results have, of course, been effective; the population has received substantial benefits and it is clear they were satisfied with the work undertaken in different neighborhoods during the first three months of Plan Bolívar 2000. Not surprisingly, the opposition and the opposition parties, on seeing the success of the plan, tried to attack the armed forces. They pointed to supposedly corrupt officials, although we know that this was a political hoax they had cooked up. Our very behavior was proof that we were working on something they had never bothered about.

And we stuck to our commitment to remain in the neighborhoods, supporting the population in tackling a social debt that had been building up for years. For example, in those Caracas neighborhoods that suffer most problems, such as a poor water supply, which they receive every 10 or 15 days, a family doesn't get enough water for their personal hygiene requirements or for preparing food.

We say here that what is most important is the conditions in which a person lives within a society. Taking all these elements into account, the government's plan, backed by the armed forces, implements a series of operations aimed at mitigating somewhat the scarcity that prevails in these areas, such as the lack of housing. Water tanks have been built or installed in homes to increase storage capacity, thereby reducing the number of days a home may be without water from 10 to 4 or 5. Of course, a special plan for maintenance work was put into effect that we called Plan Reviba, because it is a plan to repair living quarters in the poorer neighborhoods.

It is worth recalling that these neighborhoods grew in a way I would describe as uncontrolled. People seek their own solutions when a government does not provide them. People aim to satisfy their needs when a government does not satisfy them. And, of course, the population has grown over these past 40 years. We now face a situation in which Caracas has been invaded by people who are seeking a better life but who are actually living in inhuman conditions, in poor-quality housing, where they don't even have their basic needs covered.

Through a series of different initiatives the government has launched Plan Reviba and also Plan Avispa, specifically designed to overhaul existing housing and to replace unhygienic living quarters and their limited facilities with decent housing. This housing has been constructed using the experience of some Latin American and European countries that have put different ideas into practice to try and resolve housing shortages; it is a do-it-yourself system of building.

I would say that in the short time since these plans have been in operation the results have been immensely encouraging. We have seen families who are grateful to a government that has attended to their needs at a difficult time, at a time of crisis. The opposition has attacked the government, accusing it of populism, because it is working for the improvement, in one way or another, in the standard of living and life expectancy of the people.

There have been many accusations: some say that we are not united, that we are divided, split. The clearest answer we can give to this is that the armed forces are more united with each passing day. An example of this is the way we confronted the barbaric strike in December last year — the two-month fascist oil stoppage — and the coup d'état, with unity and strength.

All garrison commanders joined the plan [to combat the oil strike]. We began to hold meetings with the officials who controlled the central computer systems — computing engineers, systems network experts, and higher-level technicians — with the aim of updating them. We knew we had to be prepared to take on the duties of the PDVSA workers who were going to walk out. After completing technical preparations we focused on identifying the vulnerable aspects of the system, its reserve capacity and how a rationing plan might double this. We managed to discover how many gas pumps there were in each sector, how to distribute gas, who was responsible for each pump, and where the supply trucks were parked.

In the end this plan was carried out in its entirety, and safely, in spite of the difficulties. We gave the fascists a decisive answer even though the state lost over $10 billion on account of this wretched operation.

The coup d'état

At the time of the coup d'état I was commander of the third division. I had noticed the rising levels of tension in the city. Strikes, demonstrations, highway and road-blocks, and so on. Obviously, this was happening in the east of the city, in the wealthier neighborhoods; the poorer areas were totally calm. Remember that all this was taking place as the government was passing the 44 laws and other measures for the benefit of the people. Of course, the powerful are always in the minority, but when one of them is harmed the others also feel under attack.

At that time the mass media launched their offensive, assuming the role of the political parties. Their campaign was openly fascist, terrorist — they began to incite hatred among the population. They held a rally to launch a "*cacerolozo*" in Venezuela,[1] the same method that had been employed to overthrow [Salvador] Allende. They began to study the lives of officers, developing profiles on each of them, identifying their weaknesses, their strengths, how they could be won over. Special plans were devised for those who couldn't be convinced — to eliminate them or neutralize them.

While this was taking place, and when the atmosphere in the city was particularly tense, the top ranks of the military ordered me to carry out, with the officers in my command, tactical military operations between April 5 and 20 in the city of Vigía, Mérida. They had anticipated that the coup would take place between April 11 and 19. They also knew that my garrison would be an impediment to the coup; for this reason they gave me the orders to undertake an exercise of this type [far from the capital].

Part of my responsibilities involved the command of the garrison. However, internal order was also part of my duties, which is why I decided to ask General Lucas for authorization not to participate in the exercise. The general agreed with me, and I notified the army commander that I was not to be part of the exercise. I was initially told that this was not a problem, but then a counter-order arrived, telling me that I had to mobilize my men. I was even given the precise date on which to do this. In other words, they were paying no heed to General Lucas; they went above him and told me that I should leave Caracas. When I saw the order, I once again asked the army commander that he exempt me. He didn't reply, and since he didn't reply I interpreted his silence as his acceptance of my recommendation.

So, the morning of April 11 arrived. I was in this very office with the then minister of defense, Jorge Vicente Rangel;[2] General Lucas, a high-ranking officer; the chief of staff, Admiral Escudero; and General Vázquez Velazco. We were analyzing the situation that was being broadcast on TV.

By way of conclusion, we decided we would have to issue an official instruction telling the TV channel to calm down. At that point I noticed Dr. Jorge Vicente Rangel, who was observing the seriousness of the situation, with the demonstration at East Park heading for Miraflores Palace. Deeply concerned, he called Martel Yanier and said, in my presence, "Listen, there are around one million people at Miraflores Palace who support the president. If you allow [the counterdemonstration to continue toward the palace], we are going to end up with a confrontation, a clash between two masses of human beings. There will be thousands of deaths. Do you understand?"

At that point the decision was taken to make an official declaration in order to try to calm the population down a little. When we were going down to the TV room in the ministry, we noticed that General Vázquez Velazco had been to the bathroom on several occasions and that he was not present when the official declaration was announced.

A good while passed, we waited for him, but by then we already had our doubts. In view of his delay, there was no alternative other than to make public the message appealing to the population for calm and informing them that the armed forces were aware of what was happening. Finally, I got up and said to General Lucas, "I am going to activate Plan Ávila." This plan indicated what each of us should do [in the case of a coup attempt] and what our responsibilities were. A special mission had been devised to protect the most important facilities, particularly Miraflores Palace, the Supreme Court, and the National Assembly.

In light of what was happening, I went to the command post of the Third Division, where all the generals had gathered to watch the TV. The news programs were announcing that President Chávez had lost power because he had not met the people's expectations; that it had been inevitable something like a coup would take place. At that moment I ordered Plan Ávila to be activated — it was obvious the situation was becoming increasingly tense. We left to do the rounds of all the battalions, to get the troops armed and to call the troops to formation. We got the tanks out and equipped them with weapons and munitions. Each tank that left was headed for the courtyard of honor of the Bolívar battalion.

Around eight vehicles did not start up; we left them in the hands of the mechanic. As soon as they were put right he sent them to us. We managed to get some 40 tanks inside the palace walls. At approximately 2:30 p.m., I noticed a number of vehicles I didn't recognize had begun to enter the fort. At that moment I was told that supporters of the coup had taken the Alcabala military base, which is the link between the regional highway and the city center. They piled up cars, buses, trucks, and fuel trucks on the highway, creating chaos and blocking the road entirely.

Considering the situation, I decided to evacuate Alcabala Three and divert the remaining troops to Alcabala Two and Alcabala One.

At that point the president wanted to make contact with Rosendo

Manuel, commander of Cufa, but Manuel did not take the call. I heard all this by radio, which is when I rang the president and told him he was talking to the commander of Plan Ávila and asked him what he wanted. The following conversation then took place:

> "Well, what have you got there?"
> "I have troops available for executing Plan Ávila."
> "And the tanks?"
> "The tanks are under your orders, awaiting instructions from you."
> He immediately replied with an order, "Send me 20 tanks to reinforce security at the palace."

I met with General Silva, the tank commander. We decided to direct the tanks to the palace along a route with fewer possibilities of confrontation. The plan was carried out accordingly; the tanks left and arrived at Miraflores Palace. The coup plotters had the upper hand there, because the commander of the Ayala tank battalion was one of them and in contact with them. That was something we had been unaware of.

At this point, General Vázquez Velazco called that tank commander and told him to withdraw the tanks, which is what he did, leaving the Miraflores Palace defenseless, with no security. They seized this moment to call the president by phone and threaten him, telling him that if he didn't resign they would bomb the palace with tanks and aircraft.

During this conversation, in which they asked Chávez to step down and Chávez refused to negotiate, I was in the palace. I asked for the loan of a vehicle and headed for the fort. We had already detained the officers who had taken part in the capture of the Alcabala military bases and we were holding them in a secure place. When I entered the fort I thought I would be detained, but this did not occur. So I went to Trinidad Morán and confirmed for myself that all the officers there were in favor of the coup. They had taken the Alcabalas, and they had blocked the highway with vehicles in order to create chaos.

Once I had spoken to them and stated my position, I went to the Bolívar battalion courtyard. A commission headed by General Castillo Casto and Colonel Estúver Pineda arrived, with a group of officers and soldiers, wanting to detain me. Naturally, I took out my pistol, and told them that they knew me and that if they were thinking about detaining me then they would have to do it by force. As soon as they realized my position they calmed down a little. When I asked Colonel Montilla if a particular vehicle was his, he replied that it was. I said to him, "Come on, let's go to the palace!"

I got in and set off for Miraflores Palace. We were just about to emerge at the Paraíso area, via the second tunnel, but we saw that all the traffic had been blocked. The mayor, Leopoldo López, had used his patrols to cut it off once he found out that the tanks had left [to protect the palace]. He had taken the ignition keys from the owners of all the vehicles so that nobody could move.

We were stuck at the mouth of the tunnel, and in order not to be blocked in by the cars coming up behind us, we started flashing our headlights and did a u-turn. We parked at the cemetery so that we could go to DISIP [secret police headquarters], but unfortunately by the time we arrived the coup plotters had already taken it. In the midst of all of this, I took advantage of a misunderstanding with the DISIP director, who had been detained. He was told that I had come to pick him up to take him prisoner, and in this way we all managed to get out of the place and come here. Still, we didn't know what to do.

When we arrived [at military headquarters] I was informed that the president was here and that they wanted to talk to him. They said there was no reason to be afraid; they were going be entirely respectful toward him. They wanted me to be present, to talk to me.

But when I arrived on the fifth floor I was locked in the bathroom. They told me that the coup had been planned for years; it was the only way to ensure there would be fewer deaths. But in reality they had actually planned some deaths. They had snipers kill people from both [pro- and anti-Chávez demonstrations] in order to provoke confusion. For this reason they killed 35 human beings, fathers, boys, and girls.

All of this was told to me in the bathroom. When they finally opened the door I saw Carmona sitting in the office, in the seat of the commander-in-chief of the armed forces. Ambulance sirens were everywhere. Everyone was embracing and greeting him. Others joined in as they arrived, telling stories, rejoicing, celebrating with whiskey, champagne, while I was there watching the whole spectacle.

I knew it was my chance to leave; I was doing nothing there. I left for home but as soon I approached the elevator I saw a colonel and a general calling me over and I thought they would take me captive. As they didn't say anything, I got into the elevator and went home.

At around 7 a.m. I returned to the third division and began calling the officers to tell them to think carefully about what they were going to do, that it was important for them to understand that the president had not resigned. We were talking to them while Carmona was making his statement on TV, when he swore himself in as president and eliminated all other powers. That was when trouble started because many of the high-ranking officers had been expecting posts, which was the case for Medina Gómez, who wanted to become commander of the armed forces. On realizing this was not going to happen, he became noticeably angry. You can see this on the videotape—the look on his face indicates his regret.

We are now talking about April 12, which was when some officers realized that they had been used and, contrary to their expectations, had been removed from their posts. Annoyed, unit commanders forced a meeting the following day. They wanted an explanation, since they knew nothing about Chávez's resignation and did not agree with the idea of someone appointing himself president and eliminating all other powers.

All generals in favor of the coup were summoned to a meeting at 1 p.m. in the Ayala battalion. Nobody informed me of this meeting, but I found out about it at 11 a.m. I told the chief of military police to let everybody on the bridge pass, in other words around 400,000 people, to get them into the building where the coup supporters and the top ranks of the military were, along with Carmona. I wanted to get the people to surround the building but the chief of military police said no, he was afraid something terrible would happen. Seeing his fear, I said, "Think very carefully before denouncing me and telling them that I came here to tell you this." I was being serious when I threatened him, because I sensed the man was going to inform on me.

From there I went to where the meeting was being held. When I reached the Ayala battalion, I told the tank battalion commander, Lieutenant Colonel Cepeda Báez, to hand the tanks over to me, taking into account that I was his division commander and that the battalion was under my orders. I told him I needed to take the tanks because I wanted to deploy a strong element within the Bolívar battalion, that is, to combine infantry and tanks, allowing us to hold out until the situation had been resolved. That was my position.

He told me he couldn't give me the tanks because he was under strict orders from the army commander. I didn't want to argue with him and at any rate I began to notice that all the coup supporters, the officers and generals who backed it, were arriving. We walked into the room with all the lieutenant colonels, the same officers who had demanded an explanation, because at no point had anyone shown them the president's resignation.

I remember a young man who got up at the meeting and asked the first question, "I am here but I don't know what is going on. I haven't been shown the president's resignation and I don't agree with what is happening. All public powers and institutions have been eliminated, as have the National Assembly and the Supreme Court, and I think we need an explanation."

This led other officers to get up and criticize what had happened. General Rudy Guzmán, one of those who backed the coup, had to stand up and attempt to convince them. General Martínez Vidal took to the floor and argued that the hills were full of armed Bolivarian circles and that Chávez was guilty of all the deaths that had taken place since April 11. There was a need to change the president because Chávez had not been able to accomplish what the people demanded, which is what he had been elected for.

I got up and said, "We're all here talking and giving our assessments of the situation, but if we are going to talk to the people the first thing that must be borne in mind is that these people in the hills are armed, armed with 40 years of hunger and misery. The question we must broach here is not the question of Bolivarian circles or whether those in the hills are armed. The question we are discussing here is that an entire people is asking to see the president. Right now there are over 400,000 people outside Alcabala Three who are about to break through the barricades and go inside. The people need an answer otherwise there is going to be a civil war and it will be disastrous."

This made everyone sit down and start work on drawing up a document, which was supposedly going to be the second official declaration. They turned for guidance to General Vázquez Velazco, who was sitting beside me and who was obviously deeply embittered that he had supported the coup d'état but had not received the post he had hoped for. He was angry since the outcome of his involvement in the coup was that he was the one to be overthrown. He held no position and had been made a fool of.

At that point, General Navarro Chacón arrived, the man Carmona had appointed minister of defense, as substitute for Admiral Ramírez Pérez, who had declined the offer, suspicious of what lay ahead. When he arrived, Navarro did not wish to make a statement. He asked General Vázquez Velazco to kindly accompany him and the latter told him to wait for a moment so that he could finish writing the document. Navarro Chacón insisted on Vázquez Velazco leaving the room, but I said, "General, I would be very grateful if you could wait while General Vázquez Velazco finishes something that is important to us."

Navarro made it clear that he wanted nothing to do with me. I replied that the feeling was mutual and that I would be grateful if he left the room because we were working and he should withdraw. When they finished writing the document, Vázquez Velazco angrily handed it to me and asked for permission to talk to General Navarro, who was about 50 meters away.

Reading the document I saw that they had written incredible nonsense. I began to cross out the parts I considered inappropriate. They had written they were in agreement with the fact that Chávez had stepped down, but that they were going to reestablish civil powers. They were going to ensure the people held on to all the social welfare benefits that had been granted so far, and a whole pile of other things. We crossed out almost the entire document, leaving in small and accurate details, such as having to respect the constitution, and the importance of reestablishing the rule of law.

We were leaving some scope to the officers, but finally I stopped and said to the battalion commanders, "You are the ones who hold power; you have the weapons, the men. What are we doing sitting here? Let's go and get the general and bring him here to put an end to this once and for all. Let's try to save the people. If we don't, there will be a massacre; the troops are going to create a disaster."

We all got up and approached Navarro and Vázquez Velazco. I walked over and said, "Listen, we need to wrap this up. We can't give it any more time. There is going to be a massacre and you are the ones who are in charge of the situation." Immediately, everyone came into the room. I told Vázquez Velazco, "Read this, because we are going to talk to the press." He leafed through the document and realized I had crossed out practically everything; he looked at it and said nothing. I reminded him that he should practice reading it, because the press was coming. But I was then informed that almost all the TV relay repeater units had been removed and there were no microwave repeaters running. Images to Venezuela could only be broadcast via recorded transmissions.

Someone present pointed out that changes could be made to a recorded version by the time it was broadcast, so the truth would not be told, it would be distorted. We had to broadcast live, even if it was only the sound of one voice. A young woman from the press pointed out that we could contact a man who worked for CNN Atlanta and ask him for a link to Venezuela so our broadcast would be live. After numerous tries we made telephone contact and said, "This is a call from Venezuela, we don't want a relay broadcast. All the microwave repeaters are down here; we need you to give us a live satellite link to read the second declaration regarding the coup d'état."

Obviously, this is sensational for a journalist. So in this way we read out the second declaration, acknowledging the constitution and demanding a return to the rule of law. This is what finally turned the tables on the coup plotters. Those [military men] who had backed the coup left the room disgusted. Some of them said, "Let's go to the ministry [of defense], let's go to the ministry," which is where they all headed.

Then I went to the third division, where I was informed that a warrant for my arrest had been issued and a room in the battalion had been made ready for my imprisonment. I left and went directly to where masses of people had gathered [at the palace]. Using a war tank as a platform, I took a megaphone and right in front of the media I told the people not to leave, that it was important for them to remain. A second declaration in favor of the constitution was about to be read, and we were sure that things were going turn out okay.

I told them, "The president isn't here. They have taken him to Oxila, but all necessary steps are being taken to return him." The people applauded me and went wild. A short while later, one of them approached me and said, "They are all on the fifth floor. Why don't we take them prisoner?" I said, "Christ, that's true!"

I gathered colonels Montia Pantoja and Granadillo, looked for Ángel Albietri, and gave them instructions to enter the building. With the help of the Caracas battalion captains, they took the fifth floor of the building and detained all of them. They cut the electricity and told them they were being held prisoner for backing the coup. All their cell phones were removed. San Marino, who had been discharged from duty, was there in his uniform, as was Molina Tamayo, but Carmona was nowhere to be seen. He was in the adjoining room, and the door was closed.

The colonel knew the building. He sent the soldiers in via the rear and brought them out through the conference room, which is directly linked to the room Carmona was in. The colonel slapped Carmona on the back and told him he was under arrest for violating the constitution of the Bolivarian Republic of Venezuela. Then and there Carmona wrote out his resignation as president. I was called immediately and informed of what had taken place. I grabbed the megaphone and gave the people the news they had been waiting for.

Afterwards, all the garrisons that supported the president were called, and they gradually joined with us. We continued to inform the people that the Zulia, Barquisimeto, Carúpano, and Valencia garrisons were backing the constitution and it was this that gave us strength to go on.

At that point the atmosphere began to change. People were content, and remained so until 3:30 a.m., when news came through that the president was being brought to Miraflores Palace by helicopter. Crowds began to arrive from the valley on foot, walking along the Miraflores highway, because they wanted to see the arrival of the president.

We went to welcome him; it was a deeply moving experience, a moment of immense happiness. Everybody there was hugging each other; we saw that thanks to the efforts of the people and the armed forces we had rescued the constitution. Above all, we had rescued the dignity of an entire people, who had asked for it in the most moving way when they saw their hopes and aspirations being denied.

That is why I believe we played a vital role in this process, together with the people, because it was they who gave us the strength needed to overcome the difficulties we faced in this situation. Since then, I have always called that day the day of civil-military union and of national resurrection.

Notes

Preface

1. Hugo Chávez was first elected in 1998. In 1999 the Constituent Assembly was convened and a new constitution drafted, which was adopted after a successful referendum. Under the new constitution, a general election was called and Chávez was reelected. In April 2002 an attempted coup d'état was reversed by the people of Venezuela and the Venezuelan armed forces. In August 2004, a Recall Referendum was called by the opposition, which Chávez defeated by a large majority.

Part One

1. The full quote by Bolívar is, "Those who serve the revolution plow the sea."
2. Paraphrasing Ernesto Che Guevara in his 1965 farewell letter to his parents. See *Che Guevara Reader*, edited by David Deutschmann, New York: Ocean Press, 2003, 384.
3. Radical political party (The Radical Cause).
4. Founder of Causa R.
5. Venezuelan President 1993–98.
6. Pact signed by the Democratic Republican Union, the Christian Social Party (COPEI) and Democratic Action (AD), on October 31, 1958. The leaders of these parties committed themselves to, among other things, forming a government of national unity, whichever party triumphed

in the elections. All those who signed the pact would be included in this government's cabinet.

7. Typical dress of the plains regions.

8. Activists of the Democratic Action party (AD) are called *adecos* while those from the Christian Social party (COPEI) are called *copeyanos*.

9. Venezuelan currency.

10. The name of this tree commemorates the story of a treasonous indigenous chief allied to the Spanish conquerors. It is said that from time to time Simón Bolívar undertook excursions to the foot of the tree. It is renowned throughout Venezuela for the breadth of its branches, which stretch across 260 feet.

11. Commission responsible for administering hard currency.

12. Acosta Carles died in strange circumstances during the Caracazo.

13. Pedro Carmona, the Venezuelan businessman who briefly replaced Chávez during the April 2002 coup d'état.

14. Military command headquarters.

15. Security and Political Intelligence Service (secret police).

16. State in the plains region, Chávez's place of birth.

17. Homeland For All, a left-wing political party.

18. A weekly TV program in which Chávez and other government ministers speak about developments in Venezuela.

19. Vargas, a state in the central coastal region, was the site of widespread floods and landslides in December 1999.

20. Venzuelan Oil Limited.

21. José Antonio Paéz (1790–1873), Venezuelan soldier and politician, first president of the republic.

22. Ezequiel Zamora (1817–60), Venezuelan soldier and politican, born in Cua on February 1, 1817. He explained social unrest as a consequence of the prevailing economic crisis, due to the exploitation of the people by the Spaniards. His slogans focused on the right to land for agriculture, "free land and men," a fair distribution of wealth, the publicizing of his strong liberal ideas in the newspaper *El Venezolano*,

and his armed rising of September 7, 1848, justly earned him the title of "general of the sovereign people."

23 Birds of prey.

24. *Canalla* the original term in Spanish, a phrase commonly used to refer to socially undesirable elements.

25. Andrés Pastrana, Colombian president 1998–2002.

26. Current president of Brazil.

27. Venezuelan Corporation of Guyana.

28. The family libraries are collections of about a dozen books, supplied to families participating in Venezuela's literacy programs.

29. The first mission in Venezuela's national literacy plan, named after Simón "Robinson" Rodríguez, who was Simón Bolívar's teacher.

30. Parallel to the literacy and primary education programs of Mission Robinson, the government created Mission Ribas, named after independence hero José Felix Ribas, for individuals to complete their high school education.

31. "Don't goof around."

32. Mission Sucre, named after Marshal Antonio José de Sucre, is a scholarship program for a university education.

33. This program, with the help of over 10,000 Cuban doctors, places small community health clinics in the *barrios*, or neighborhoods, in areas that previously never had doctors nearby.

34. Plan to incorporate the unemployed in different areas of nation's economic, social, and cultural structures, using local resources, sustainable techniques, and cooperative organization.

35. During Aleida Guevara's visit to Venezuela, she conducted several interviews in the Venezuelan press and on TV, suggesting Chávez had been too soft on opponents such as those who executed the failed 2002 coup d'état.

36. Camilo Cienfuegos, commander in the Rebel Army that defeated Batista's dictatorship in Cuba in 1959.

37. Food markets set up in poorer neighborhoods, where food is subsidized.

38. This referendum was finally held on August 15, 2004. Hugo Chávez won by a majority of 58.25 percent, according to data provided by the National Electoral Council.

39. Regional elections were held on October 31, 2004, in which the coalition of Bolivarian forces gained 20 of the governments under dispute.

40. Tomás Borge, *Face to Face with Fidel Castro*, New York: Ocean Press, 1993. Originally published in Spanish in 1992 as *Un grano de maíz*.

Part Two

1. Current chief of the National Defense Command.

2. General Raúl Isaías Baduel, Venezuela's current army commander.

3. Member of the Miasanta commando group.

4. Popular folk music that originated in Mexico.

5. Folk music of the Venezuelan plains region.

6. A second military uprising against the government of Carlos Andrés Pérez.

7. Five Cuban men, known around the world as the Cuban Five, are currently serving lengthy sentences in US prisons, on trumped-up charges of conspiracy to commit treason and conspiracy to commit murder. They were monitoring the Miami-based extremist groups that conduct terrorist activities against Cuba.

8. Shock troops used during Pinochet's regime to terrorize the people.

9. The Sao Paolo Forum is a collective of Latin American left-wing parties.

10. Hugo Chávez, *El golpe fascista contra Venezuela*, Havana: Ediciones Plaza, 2003.

11. Fidel Castro, "History Will Absolve Me," in *Fidel Castro Reader*, forthcoming from Ocean Press.

12. Fidel Castro, *Fidel and Religion: Conversations with Frei Betto*, New York: Ocean Press, 1990. Originally published in Spanish in 1985 as *Fidel y la religión*.

13. Gianni Minà *An Encounter with Fidel*, New York: Ocean Press, 1991. Originally published in Spanish in 1991 as *Un encuentro con Fidel*.

14. Political discussions broadcast on Cuban TV every weekday evening.

15. In Latin America the Free Trade Area of the Americas (FTAA) is known as the Acuerdo Libre de Comercio para las Americas (ALCA). FTAA-Lite, or the little ALCA, is known as ALQUITA.

16. The Caribbean Community.

17. *Lampiño* is the Spanish term for men who lack or have no body hair.

Appendix One

1. See Part Two in the book for this interview, held on February 10, 2004.

Appendix Two

1. The "banging of the pots," a means of protest of the middle and upper classes, used in Chile against the popular government of Salvador Allende.

2. Current vice-president of Venezuela.

CHE GUEVARA READER

Writings on Politics and Revolution

Edited by David Deutschmann

This new edition of the bestselling *Che Guevara Reader* features the most complete selection of Guevara's writings, letters and speeches available in English. It includes essays on the Cuban revolutionary war and guerrilla warfare, his analysis of the first years of the Cuban Revolution and his vision for Latin America and the Third World.

ISBN 1-876175-69-9 *(Also available in Spanish 1-876175-93-1)*

LATIN AMERICA

Awakening of a Continent

Ernesto Che Guevara

This book presents Che's overall vision for Latin America: from his youthful travels until his death in Bolivia. Here, the reader can observe Che's development from spectator to participant in the struggles of Latin America, and finally to theoretician of the Latin American reality.

ISBN 1-920888-38-1 *(Also available in Spanish 1-876175-71-0)*

SELF-PORTRAIT

Ernesto Che Guevara

Self-Portrait, an intimate look at the man behind the icon, is a remarkable photographic and literary memoir, drawing on the rich seam of diaries, letters, poems, journalism, and short stories Che Guevara left behind him in Cuba. Compiled in close collaboration with his family, this book reveals Che's extraordinary candor, irony, dry humor, and passion.

ISBN 1-876175-82-6, 305 pages, photos throughout

(Also available in Spanish 1-876175-89-3)

GLOBAL JUSTICE

Liberation and Socialism

Ernesto Che Guevara

Is there an alternative to the neoliberal globalization ravaging our planet? Collected here are three of Guevara's classic works, presenting his revolutionary view of a different world in which human solidarity and understanding replace imperialist aggression and exploitation.

ISBN 1-876175-45-1 *(Also available in Spanish 1-876175-46-X)*

CHE: A MEMOIR BY FIDEL CASTRO

Preface by Jesús Montané

For the first time Fidel Castro writes with candor and affection of his relationship with Ernesto Che Guevara, documenting his extraordinary bond with Cuba from the revolution's early days to the final guerrilla expeditions to Africa and Bolivia.

ISBN 1-920888-25-X *(Also available in Spanish 1-875284-83-4)*

MANIFESTO

Three Classic Essays on How to Change the World

Ernesto Che Guevara, Rosa Luxemburg, Karl Marx and Friedrich Engels

"If you are curious and open to the life around you, if you are troubled as to why, how and by whom political power is held and used... if your curiosity and openness drive you toward wishing to 'do something,' you already have much in common with the writers of the essays in this book."

—Adrienne Rich, from her preface to *Manifesto*

ISBN 1-876175-98-2 *(Also available in Spanish 1-876175-13-6)*

CAPITALISM IN CRISIS

Globalization and World Politics Today

Fidel Castro

Cuba's leader adds his voice to the growing international chorus against neo-liberalism and globalization. Includes Fidel's 1999 speech in Venezuela soon after the election of Hugo Chávez as president.

ISBN 1-876175-18-4

WAR, RACISM AND ECONOMIC INJUSTICE

The Global Ravages of Capitalism

Fidel Castro

A tireless advocate for a more just world, Fidel Castro analyzes the crisis of the Third World, possibilities for sustainable development and outlines Cuba's response to the 9/11 terrorist attacks. Includes a speech made by Fidel Castro in the Venezuelan National Assembly, comparing the two nations' constitutions and analyzing the Bolivarian Revolution.

ISBN 1-876175-47-8

WARS OF THE 21ST CENTURY
New Threats, New Fears
Ignacio Ramonet

An activist intellectual like Noam Chomsky, Ignacio Ramonet is the internationally recognized and respected editor of the prestigious *Le Monde diplomatique*. For the first time this articulate and radical voice is presented to English-language readers, discussing the fundamental global issues at stake in the recent wars in Iraq, Afghanistan, Kosovo and elsewhere.

ISBN 1-876175-96-6

THE CUBA PROJECT
CIA Covert Operations 1959-62
Fabián Escalante

"Fabián Escalante is in a unique position to add significant insight and information about this crucial chapter of modern history. His review of CIA covert operations against Cuba is to be greatly welcomed, and should be widely read—and pondered." —Noam Chomsky

ISBN 1-876175-99-0

COVERT ACTION
The Roots of Terrorism
Edited by Ellen Ray and William H. Schaap

With an introduction written during the war on Iraq, this book brings together a selection of key articles from the authoritative magazine *CovertAction*, presenting a comprehensive background to the terrorist attacks of September 11, 2001, and the current "war on terror."

ISBN 1-876175-84-2

WHAT EVERY RADICAL NEEDS TO KNOW ABOUT STATE REPRESSION
A Guide for Activists
Victor Serge
Introduction by Dalia Hashad

Serge's exposé of the surveillance and harassment of political activists by the Czarist police reads like a spy thriller. But as Dalia Hashad describes in her introduction, this book resonates against a new wave of repression and racial profiling post-September 11.

ISBN 1-920888-17-9

CHILE: THE OTHER SEPTEMBER 11

An Anthology of Reflections on the 1973 Coup in Chile

Edited by Pilar Aguilera and Ricardo Fredes

Contributions by Ariel Dorfman, Salvador Allende, Pablo Neruda, Víctor and Joan Jara, Beatriz Allende, Fidel Castro and others.

ISBN 1-876175-50-8

SALVADOR ALLENDE READER

Chile's Voice of Democracy

Edited by James Cockcroft and Jane Carolina Canning

On September 11, 1973, General Augusto Pinochet led a bloody coup against President Salvador Allende in Chile, backed and financed by the United States. Striking parallels with Venezuela today make this a compelling and important read, with Allende himself describing how Chileans struggled against all-powerful U.S. and transnational corporations in their efforts to achieve democratic socialism.

ISBN 1-876175-24-9

LATIN AMERICA

From Colonization to Globalization

Noam Chomsky in conversation with Heinz Dieterich

An indispensable book for those interested in Latin America and the politics and history of the region. As Latin America hovers on the brink of a major social and economic crisis, internationally acclaimed philosopher, scholar and political activist Noam Chomsky discusses some of the principal political events in recent years.

ISBN 1-876175-13-3

CENTURY OF TERROR IN LATIN AMERICA

A Chronicle of U.S. Crimes Against Humanity

Luis Suárez

From the Monroe Doctrine through the "dirty wars" in Cuba and Central America, and the neoliberal agenda being imposed with such explosive consequences today, this is a comprehensive history of U.S. intervention in Latin America.

ISBN 1-920888-37-3